Professional Development in the Lifelong Learning Sector

m
LearningMatters

First published in 2007 by Learning Matters Ltd.

British Library Cataloguing in Publication Data
A CIP record for this book is available from the British Library.

ISBN: 978 1 84445 083 1

Cover and text design by Topics – The Creative Partnership
Project management by Deer Park Productions, Tavistock, Devon
Typeset by Pantek Arts Ltd, Maidstone, Kent
Printed and bound in Great Britain by Cromwell Press, Trowbridge, Wiltshire

Learning Matters Ltd
33 Southernhay East
Exeter EX1 1NX
Tel: 01392 215560
info@learningmatters.co.uk
www.learningmatters.co.uk

Contents

Acknowledgements   iv

Introduction   1

1   Are leaders born or made?   7

2   Connecting with people   20

3   Instinct for opportunity   35

4   Telling a compelling story   45

5   Developing self and teams 1: reflective leadership   57

6   Developing self and teams 2: creating capability   67

7   Making things happen   81

8   Staying positive   94

9   Flexibility in leading change   105

10   Joined-up leadership   119

Appendix: Winterhill College organisation chart   132

References and further reading   133

Index   136

Acknowledgements

Many people helped in the research for this book. The authors would particularly like to thank the following:

Charles Bartholomew, Programme Manager, Music and Performing Arts, Stoke-on-Trent College

Ken Burgess, Head of Faculty for Engineering and Construction, Stoke-on-Trent College

Jackie Fisher, Principal and Chief Executive, Newcastle College

John Fitzpatrick, Programme Leader, Lincoln College

Derek Howsham, Programme Leader, Lincoln College

Graham Moore, Principal and Chief Executive, Stoke-on-Trent College

Ioan Morgan, Principal and Chief Executive, Warwickshire College

Steve Shobrook, Head of School, Lincoln College

Carol Thomas, Head of Faculty for Caring and Service Industries, Stoke-on-Trent College

Kevin Williams, Head of School, Lincoln College

Introduction

Imagine you have been given the time and leisure to spend a day wandering around a busy Further Education (FE) college in the Lifelong Learning sector. You decide to use this opportunity to see what issues are facing people in leadership roles at various levels within the organisation. So, as well as finding the time to complete an increasing load of paperwork, what else are these leaders doing? Over there is a Head of Section trying to prepare feedback and organise support for a member of his team who is struggling with classroom management. Down the corridor is a Head of School about to chair a meeting about retention and achievement figures and wondering how to encourage her team to improve their performance without appearing to 'blame' them. On another part of the campus a Head of Faculty is planning for the merger of two schools under his leadership as part of a response to the Train to Gain initiative and to competition within the local training market. In a crowded staff workroom a Subject Leader ploughs through a new set of national standards and tries to work out the best way to update and reassure her team. And at the top of the building, in his tastefully decorated office, the Principal contemplates his approaching retirement and questions the success of his current strategy for building leadership capacity within the college.

This book is written for all those leaders and more. It addresses leadership issues that arise for those at the very top of senior leadership teams as well as for the lecturer who leads a subject team of two or three colleagues. Most of the examples and case studies focus on middle and first-line leaders, not least because there are so many of us out there! It has been estimated that currently, in FE colleges alone, up to one in seven staff have a leadership and management role (*Times Educational Supplement*, 7 July 2006). If we also count first-line leadership roles such as subject leader – and indeed so we should – the proportion is probably even higher. This means that leadership skills are now more important to the sector than ever before, and this is clearly reflected in recent government policy and legislation.

This introduction is designed to explain:

- who this book is aimed at;
- what it sets out to do and why;
- the current context in which team leaders at all levels in FE are operating;
- the key arguments about leadership which this book sets out;
- the focus of each chapter;
- how you can use the book to support your professional development.

Leadership: the Occupational Standards

Since 1999 we have had Occupational Standards for leadership and management in the post-compulsory Learning and Skills sector. For the sake of brevity, we shall refer to the current standards (LLUK, 2006) in this book as the *Leadership and Management Standards*, or sometimes simply as the *Standards*. They identify three levels at which leadership operates: first line, middle and senior level; and they set out four key areas for development (strategic practice, learning and the learning environment, leading teams and individuals, and managing finance and resources). In addition, they present the key values and assumptions on which the standards are based, and make it clear that there are three pillars which support leadership performance. (1) relevant knowledge; (2) the ability to evaluate and apply that knowledge; and (3) the necessary skills and qualities of leadership. If we add all this together, our basic ingredients for leadership performance look something like this:

- Leadership values
- Leadership knowledge
- Evaluation and appropriate application of leadership knowledge
- Leadership skills
- Leadership qualities

Throughout this book you will see that we refer to these ingredients, both in our analysis of theory and in our building of leadership models. This enables you to refer back and forth between the book and standards if you so wish, in order to track or evaluate your professional development. You will see, too, in the chapters which follow, that – in line with the standards – we place a strong emphasis on *values*, or what is sometimes referred to as the 'moral compass', as being very much at the heart of all leadership decision-making.

The Association for College Management (ACM) has developed materials to help those with leadership and management roles in FE to carry out self-assessment against the Standards as part of their professional development (ACM, 2005). Self-assessment, of course, requires us to reflect on our professional practice, and so you will find an emphasis in this book on reflection and reflective leadership practice. You'll be asked to critically analyse and evaluate not only your own skills and qualities but also the performance of some of the fictional characters you'll find here. These range from subject leaders to principals. Some of them lead their teams very effectively, while others – as you'll discover – still have a long way to go.

White Paper: *Raising Skills, Improving Life Chances*

This White Paper (DfES, 2006) was an important milestone for the Lifelong Learning sector and is of particular significance for leaders at all levels in FE colleges. As well as endorsing the recommendation of the Foster Report (2005) that FE's mission be clearly focused on delivering skills to support the economy, this White Paper sets out, among a whole raft of other strategies, the necessity for colleges to develop specialist areas, the requirement for all staff to undertake annual continuing professional development (CPD), and for newly appointed principals to gain a qualification in leadership.

It is clear from this that leadership is under the spotlight – and for good reason. The implementation of the strategies set out in the White Paper will challenge leaders at every level as they endeavour to support and motivate their team through what may, in some cases, be radical changes in their workload, their professional practice and their sense of purpose. It seems likely that the mandatory CPD will focus on equipping increasing numbers of staff with the leadership skills appropriate to both their current level and the level to which they aspire. This is all part of building leadership capacity and expertise within the sector. As one of the principals we interviewed commented: *Nobody in this organisation will go through a day without displaying leadership.* This confirms what many of us have long observed: that if you work in FE you're sure to find yourself needing leadership skills.

Policy and practice: the current context in which leaders lead

Another of the White Paper's reforms has been the setting up of the Learning and Skills Council's new Framework for Excellence, which proposes new performance indicators for measuring a college's effectiveness across three areas: responsiveness (learner and employer satisfaction), quality (including achievement rates) and the control and health of finances. This has been greeted with limited enthusiasm by the sector, where concerns continue to be expressed by those in leadership roles at all levels about what is seen as increasing bureaucracy. Also part of the current context in which FE leaders operate are the initiatives of the Quality Improvement Agency (QIA), which was set up in 2005 to take a lead in the drive to raise standards in the Lifelong Learning sector and promote self-improvement in colleges. Included in its measures are a network of advisors who will help colleges tailor their provision to the needs of employers and their local community, and an online facility for colleges to share best practice.

In a book about leadership and leading teams within this sector it is important that we bear in mind this context within which leaders operate. As the 2006 White Paper illustrates very well, it is a context of frequent change, both in policy and practice, and one in which leaders can become easily caught up in being 'responsive' rather than creative, reactive rather than proactive. This is a leadership dilemma which we explore in some depth in Chapter 9.

Current issues for leaders in FE

When we asked leaders at various levels in FE to identify the leadership issues that loomed most important for them in their professional role they presented us with a list that ranged from the philosophical – how to arrive at a consensus about the purposes of FE – to the purely practical – how to prioritise when snowed under with paperwork. Their list also included questions about how to reconcile heavy responsibility with lack of executive power, how to balance 'quality' with 'viability'; how to win credibility and trust from their team; and how to enthuse and motivate their team in the face of continuous change and the necessities of bureaucratic monitoring.

Interestingly, the first-line leaders we spoke to, as well as those in senior leadership roles, including principals, identified many of the same concerns. Published research also spotlights identical issues as a source of concern for team leaders at various levels in colleges (for example: Lumby and Tomlinson; 2000; Withers; 2000 and Briggs; 2001). As a result, we've taken these themes and woven them into the scenarios and case studies which you'll find in the chapters that follow, in order to explore and evaluate ways in which leadership theory can be applied to cope with, address or even resolve these key dilemmas. We argue that there is no universally 'correct' leadership style (a view again supported by recent research (LSDA, 2005)), but rather that leaders need to develop a repertoire of skills and qualities together with a critical understanding which will allow them to adapt their approach as the situation demands.

What you'll find in this book

So we have taken these leadership issues and developmental needs, identified for us by team leaders in FE at all levels, and used them as our starting point. Our purpose has been not only to suggest ways in which leaders can develop and enhance those skills and qualities necessary for effective leadership, but also – and most importantly – to encourage the reader to analyse and reflect upon how those skills and qualities might apply in practical leadership situations. You'll find that this book takes an interactive and lively approach, presenting you with scenarios in which you can test your own leadership skills and knowledge as well as evaluating those of our cast of imaginary leaders in our fictional organisation 'Winterhill College'. This fictional college forms the backdrop to all the scenarios in each chapter, thereby enabling us, and you, to keep a whole-college perspective even when evaluating situations at a micro level. It also helps set the issues we address firmly in the current context of the Lifelong Learning sector, with all its background of policy imperatives and continuous change which we've touched on in this introduction.

You'll find that our key words in this book are *excellence*, *authenticity* and *joined-up leadership*. Our purpose is to demonstrate ways in which FE leaders at all levels can achieve and build on the base-line 'competencies' of the occupational standards in order to achieve a leadership style and level of skills and understanding *appropriate to their own personality and their own role*.

In the first part of the book we talk about the overall structure of the text and how it relates to the context of Lifelong Learning, and we introduce the main themes, including an exploration in Chapter 1 of whether effective leaders are born or made. We argue that the question may be a misleading one, particularly at this time and in this sector when there is increasing emphasis upon professional development in leadership skills.

In the second part of the book we take a number of leadership themes and explore them in detail. In Chapter 2 we focus on what is perhaps the most important leadership skill of all: connecting and communicating effectively with those we lead and generating a sense of teamwork. Chapter 3 turns our attention outwards, from the team to the wider environment and the issue of responsiveness, and looks at how we can develop the instinct, so valuable in a leader at any level, for reading the situation and spotting an opportunity. In Chapter 4 we look at ways in which we can make work meaningful for our team, how we can communicate a collective vision and purpose. We call this chapter 'Telling a compelling story'. Chapters 5 and 6 reflect the area of the occupational standards which is about developing self and teams, and their focus is upon how we can develop ourselves as leaders and how we can create capability within our team through strategies such as mentoring and modelling good practice. Chapter 7 tackles that essential facet of the leadership role: taking action and getting results, while Chapter 8 explores ways in which we can keep our team feeling positive, even in the face of setbacks.

In the final part we provide you with the opportunity to apply these themes in an integrated way to a range of leadership challenges. So, for example, in Chapter 9 we turn to that perennial issue of change: how we respond to it, facilitate it, and lead our teams safely through it. And in Chapter 10, we encourage you to try out your own skills of 'joined up' leadership by analysing a series of dilemmas faced by leaders at various levels within an FE college, and applying what you have learnt from the preceding chapters to come up with a solution or at least some friendly advice.

How to use this book

This will depend very much on your purpose. If you are reading it as part of a CPD programme you'll find guidance at the beginning of each chapter which will help you to link the contents to the Occupational Standards for Leadership and Management and also to identify the chapter contents in terms of learning outcomes. Our advice would be to read the chapters through in sequence, engaging with the Tasks and Discussions so that you can evaluate your own progress and follow the key arguments and ideas as they develop. However, it may be that you occasionally find it useful to read the chapters in a different order so as to match the sequencing of the CPD programme you're following. For example, you may need to focus in initially on 'leading change' or on 'developing teams'. We would suggest, however, that you begin in any case with Chapter 1, as this sets out the themes and the context for all that follows. At the end of Chapters 2 to 8 you will find a section headed 'Self-evaluation and development'. This presents you with the opportunity to reflect on how the ideas in the chapter can be applied and evaluated in terms of your own leadership performance and role. Chapters 9 and 10, in their entirety, present extended opportunities for this. Also towards the end of Chapters 2 to 8 you will find a section headed 'The dark side'. This casts a critical eye on some of the pitfalls which leaders must endeavour to avoid.

And finally...

In researching and preparing for this book it has been our privilege to engage in conversation with some of the finest leaders in the sector, from principals to heads of school, from faculty heads to leaders of subject teams. Their insights and advice have enabled us to keep this book grounded in the real world of further education and lifelong learning. It remains for us to wish you, the reader, well, and to hope that you will find this book useful in supporting your own continuing professional development.

1. Are leaders born or made?

CHAPTER OBJECTIVES

This chapter is designed to help you to:

- define what makes an effective leader;
- consider the role of 'competencies' in leadership development;
- reflect upon the idea that some aspects of leadership may be hard to learn;
- examine the benefits of having variety rather than homogeneity in leadership approaches;
- consider the place of excellence and authenticity in the development of leadership skills and styles.

Introduction

What was that question again? Are leaders born or made? Well, your life is no doubt stressful enough. So, to avoid keeping you in suspense any longer than is necessary, the answer is: yes and no.

To be honest with you, we have no real intention of providing a definitive answer to this question, because for us it is the wrong question to be trying to answer. In which case, you may be forgiven for wondering at this point why we have devoted an entire chapter to it.

The question of whether leaders are born or made may ultimately be pointless, but exploring it allows us to touch briefly upon a whole range of more germane questions about leadership, which we then go on to look at in further detail throughout the rest of the book. This serves as a very useful 'taster', then, for many of our recurring themes. These include:

- the leadership persona – charisma and personality in leadership;
- authenticity and its role in building trust;
- instinct and intuition in leadership;
- diversity and individuality versus standardisation and consistency;
- the effectiveness of current management development approaches;
- the role of collaborative leadership;
- how leaders connect with people and win followers;
- learning and leadership;
- the role of storytelling in leadership.

It's interesting to reflect that 25 years ago – within the living career memory of some current FE colleagues – such discourses about the skills and qualities of leaders and managers in the sector would have seemed something of a novelty. The organisational focus was often still on the quality of people's teaching and training even when it came to making appointments to leadership roles. This meant that a head of section or head of department could rise to this position through having a reputation as an excellent teacher rather than through any demonstration of leadership or organisational ability. As a consequence, many newly promoted leaders found themselves having to learn on the job, with greater or lesser degrees of success. Given that this was in the days before mandatory training for FE teachers (let alone leaders), we could begin to wonder whether there was a common assumption at that time that someone could be a 'born' teacher or leader and that both possessed exactly the same set of qualities and skills.

But this assumption – that effective teacher = effective leader – couldn't long survive the impact of incorporation in 1993. In their new identity as accountable corporate bodies handling multi-million pound budgets, colleges began a rapid move towards a business model in terms of management structures and roles. As we saw in the Introduction, it was not until 2002 that national occupational standards were developed for leadership and management in the post-compulsory sector, although the intervening years saw a growing recognition that these roles called for specialised qualities and skills. This change of approach – from assuming that effective teachers will make effective leaders to the introduction of national standards – seems to reflect a move away from the 'leaders are born' to the 'leaders can be made' argument.

Leadership development in the Learning and Skills sector

A 2003 Learning and Skills Development Agency (LSDA) survey found that, across the Learning and Skills sector, professional development in leadership and management was still not considered a high priority. In fact, the greatest obstacle identified to effective professional development for leadership was lack of time. This suggests a continuing pattern of 'learning on the job' rather than formalised training. But even though new appointments to leadership roles in FE, particularly in first-line management, can still find themselves picking up the necessary skills as they go along, they do now have a set of standardised criteria against which to measure their performance, in the form of the Leadership and Management Standards (see below). Perhaps significantly, considerably more junior and middle managers (as opposed to senior managers) indicate an interest in gaining some professional development in this field (LSDA, 2003). The three leadership activities which the respondents to the survey considered to be of prime importance were:

● monitoring and developing team and individual performance;

● building and maintaining productive working relationships;

● managing change and continuous improvement.

It's interesting to note here that two of the three are exclusively about skills with people, and we'll be picking that point up again in the chapters that follow.

Most recently, as we go to press, the White Paper, *Further Education: Raising Skills, Improving Life Chances* (DfES, 2006) contains the proposal that all new college principals should gain a leadership qualification, an indication, perhaps, that even those 'born to lead' may need a little help in perfecting their leadership skills!

Competent leadership and the National Standards

The National Standards set out criteria for 'competent' leadership and management at three operational levels: first line, middle and senior management. Like other sets of occupational competencies, the National Standards also include relevant areas of skills and knowledge. In this sense, the Standards can be referred to as a 'competence-based' model. Such a model has distinct advantages for the sector as it is currently constituted. These advantages include: *clarity, consistency, accessibility, professionalisation and non-alignment in the 'born or made'* debate. Let's have a look at each of these in more detail.

Clarity. The standards set out clearly the role and function of leadership and management in the sector. At all three operational levels, these are structured into four key areas:

- A: Developing strategic practice
- B: Developing and sustaining learning and the learning environment
- C: Leading teams and individuals
- D: Managing finance and resources.

In a rapidly developing sector where many managers and leaders had little formal training relevant to their role, the introduction of a competence model with its clear presentation of the skills and qualities required can be seen as a real progression from the previous 'model', which was often a case of 'picking it up as you go along'.

Consistency. Competence-based standards provide the framework for establishing a degree of standardisation – institutionally, regionally and nationally – of management and leadership performance in the sector. Such consistency of base-line standards encourages confidence in the sector from learners, employers and other stakeholders.

Accessibility. The competence model, while fixed in terms of outcomes, allows for the greatest possible flexibility in terms of modes of learning, in individual starting points, in sequencing and in duration. For example, where one section leader in an FE college may choose to undertake a part-time Masters degree in educational leadership which addresses all aspects of the standards and takes two years to complete, another may opt for a less formalised approach of self-assessment, including drawing on previous experience of leadership gained in a commercial organisation, and yet another might choose a reflective approach which includes mentor support.

Professionalisation. A national framework of leadership and management competencies, knowledge and skills helps to establish for leaders in the sector not only a clear sense of role identity, but also a professional credibility within that role.

Non-alignment. In terms of the question with which we began this chapter, the competence model doesn't align itself firmly with either side of the 'born or made' argument. It allows for accreditation of existing competence but also for training on the job, A 'born' leader would presumably be able to demonstrate easily that she meets all the standards without the need for professional training or intervention. The leader in the making, on the other hand, would have a clear idea of which competencies, skills and areas of knowledge needed further development.

Of course, nothing is entirely straightforward! In reading through these advantages, it may have occurred to you that the competence model can have some drawbacks, too.

TASK

Let's listen in now on part of a performance management discussion between Lilly, Head of School of Communication, and Graham, one of her heads of section.

Lilly *OK, Graham, we've spent a little time discussing what might be helpful objectives for you in the coming twelve months, and how these fit with my overall strategy for the faculty and the challenges I see us facing next year. What I want to explore with you now is your own personal and professional development needs against this background.*

Graham *Yeah, sure. (He struggles to dig a lever arch file from his briefcase.). I've been assessing myself against the competency framework . . .*

Lilly *That's very impressive. Which one?*

Graham *Ah, well . . . That's where it got a bit tricky. I thought I was doing quite well against the LLUK [Lifelong Learning UK] leadership and management standards. I'd ticked most of those boxes. But I'm not sure how the CEL [Centre for excellence in Leadership] leadership qualities fit into this, and then I realised the ACM Self-Assessment took a reflective approach. Of course, having been involved with our Every Child Matters initiative, I should perhaps have had a look at the Website, because I believe they're producing some guidance on leadership for local champions . . .*

> | Lilly | *Yes, OK, Graham. I think I get the point you're trying to make here. Have you managed to identify anything useful for analysing your own development needs?* |
> | --- | --- |
> | Graham | *Oh, well, yes . . . (finally managing to extricate the file from the briefcase) . . . It's all good stuff, you know. Can't really argue with any of it really. It's just that, well, you know . . .* |
> | Lilly | *Yes, go on. What exactly?* |
> | Graham | *Well, my Auntie Jean, she used to be on the stage, when she was a teenager, back in the days before Vaudeville finally died. She played all the seaside resorts. Being on stage sort of ran in that branch of the family, and her parents helped develop her act.* |
> | Lilly | *Mmm, don't want to rush you, Graham, but I've a meeting in an hour. Is this going anywhere?* |
> | Graham | *Yes. You see at first her act was tap-dancing, then they thought of getting her to tap-dance en pointe. Once she'd mastered this, they persuaded her to tap-dance en pointe while playing the accordion. Auntie Jean finally decided to jack it all in when her parents suggested that while tap-dancing en pointe and playing the accordion she could strap some cymbals to her knees and play those as well.* |
> | Lilly | *And . . . ?* |
> | Graham | *Well, when I look at these competencies, I feel a bit like that myself . . .* |

Consider for a moment what may be the drawbacks of a purely competence-based model of leadership. You might like to note down your ideas and then read on to compare them with ours.

DISCUSSION

So, in management and leadership development circles, why has a certain air of caution started to creep into the otherwise enthusiastic and seemingly unstoppable spread of the competency culture? We detect four main reasons for this. We'll call them the four Cs.

- Comprehensiveness – can every aspect of leadership be reduced to a learned behaviour?
- Cloning – if leadership can be so prescribed, why are successful leaders all so very different in personality and approach? Where does this leave personal style?
- Common sense – has this analytical approach to defining an ever more bewildering array of leadership skills and behaviours knocked all the common sense out of leadership development?

● Classical perfection – in our desire for consistency and control, have we foisted upon managers, like Graham, so complete an ideal of the perfect leader that no one can ever hope to attain it?

Let's look at each of these arguments in more detail.

Comprehensiveness

How reasonable is it to put forward a framework of leadership that prescribes all of the necessary behaviours and invites us to learn them?

TASK

Look at the following list and write against each item whether you feel it is wholly learned, partly innate or wholly innate (that is to say you've either got it or you haven't). What evidence from your own experience or from wider reading would you present to support your view? You might like to make some notes that you can return to when you've read further, to see whether your view changes as you reflect on what you read.

1. Articulate a clear vision and purpose to your team.

2. Inspire people to follow you and win their loyalty and trust.

3. Anticipate and sense opportunities for change and improvement.

4. Develop others through constructive feedback and coaching.

DISCUSSION

It is true that we can observe leaders and clearly see whether they practise specific behaviours that have been identified as successful. We can assess the extent to which someone is able to *articulate a clear vision* of the future to their team, and we can even assess the team's understanding of that vision. Not only that, but we can reasonably claim to be able to help leaders learn how to practise this behaviour more often or more effectively. Likewise, we can learn how to *give feedback and coach people* more expertly (although, even here, there are those who might argue that some people are 'born coaches'). The same is true of many aspects of leadership, from improved interpersonal skills to managing physical and financial resources.

But equally, there are leadership success factors that are at best only partly ascribable to learned behaviour. Some leaders, in communicating their vision, will be more motivating, *inspiring trust and loyalty* more naturally than others. You can probably think of examples from your own experience of leaders whose vision and enthusiasm were inspirational, and others whose style or manner made theirs less so. Was this about communication technique or the person involved, their warmth or humanity? In analysing the vast array of leadership studies and models already in print, a recent research team found only two common factors which linked all of these hundreds of recipes for leadership (Nohria et al., 2003).

The first of these was the ability to *connect with people* at a very personal level. As we saw earlier, the LSDA found that 'people skills' are seen as a priority for those undertaking leadership development in FE. But it would seem fair to suggest that this ability to 'connect' with people entails more than a collection of interpersonal techniques. There are those individuals whom we naturally warm to, and who are able to inspire a degree of trust and even affection very quickly. Emotional intelligence presumably has a role to play here. How much of this can really be taught?

The second common factor Nohria and his team found was having a great *instinct for anticipating opportunities and change*. Significantly, in our own research with leaders in FE, we have found that an instinct for opportunity seems to be a common requirement for leaders at all levels. This is the knack of constantly scanning the community/marketplace for opportunities to develop or adjust course provision in order to meet new needs and bring in more business. It can happen at college, faculty or programme level, and it is more than simple data collection. It is a partly intuitive process by which leaders enable the college to continuously and successfully adjust, by recognising, and even anticipating, potential opportunities in provision. This, of course, is a quality long-recognised in successful entrepreneurs and increasingly featuring in mainstream leadership studies. The importance of 'adaptive leadership', the ability to see connections and find meaning in the ever-changing circumstances which face us, is complemented by an increased focus on intuition and sensing situations (Goffee and Jones, 2000);(Heifetz and Laurie, 1997); (Lipman-Blumen, 2002). Again, to what extent can this instinct be learned?

Finally, under this heading of *Comprehensiveness*, to what extent can leaders really learn to be more 'transformational'? As we explained in our introduction, the Learning and Skills Research Centre has identified transformational leadership as being more effective than other styles in the Lifelong Learning sector (Lumby et al., 2005). Research from the US, which has explored what lies behind transformational leadership behaviour, shows that emotional recognition and personality traits, in particular agreeableness, are linked positively to transformational leadership behaviour (Judge and Bono, 2000; Rubin et al., 2005). High extraversion, for example, was found to lead to transformational behaviour, provided it was combined with emotional intelligence, whereas high extraversion/low emotional intelligence leaders tended to be perceived as insensitive and 'all talk'. We can present it in a simple form like this:

extravert + high emotional intelligence = transformational behaviour
extravert + low emotional intelligence = insensitive and 'all talk'

We'll be talking more about emotional intelligence in future chapters, But even if we argue that emotional intelligence can be learned to a degree, all the management development in the world will not make an introvert into an extravert.

Cloning

Even the most superficial study of successful leaders, whether world-renowned or working away in our own organisations, will reveal a glorious variety of personalities, styles and idiosyncrasies. This is presumably not because the competency police have yet to finish the job of getting everyone in line, but rather because variety is what works. Indeed, what marks out the most successful leaders is an authenticity that stems from this fit between their natural preferences and the way they lead. In other words, they tend to lead from their own personality and style, rather than trying to be someone they are not. Of course, this is not a straightforward either/or choice. Having a style of our own does not preclude learning helpful behaviours from leadership development or role models, but what we see in the most successful leaders is an ability to integrate this into their own leadership persona.

The danger, then, is that an over-reliance on a competency-based approach can result in inauthentic leadership and a presumption of managerial control, which, at the extremes, inclines us to 'one-size-fits-all' development approaches and a tendency to always fit the person to the job rather than the other way around. It may lead us to ignore the impact of environment and circumstances on the sort of leader we are. Bennis writes of leaders being forged in the 'crucible' of circumstances by a combination of their own personal qualities, and the way in which they make meaning of their experiences (Bennis and Thomas, 2002).

> own personal qualities + the circumstances in which we lead + the meaning we make of our experiences = style of leadership

This urge to standardise may also tempt us into the trap of 'remedial' management development. By this we mean the tendency to assess development needs according to which bits of the competency model seem to be missing, and to attempt to 'plug these gaps' in the individual's performance.

Let's consider Lilly again, whom we met earlier. As head of school she has a range of responsibilities across all four of the key areas of the National Standards: developing strategic practice; developing and sustaining learning and the learning environment; leading teams and individuals; and managing finance and resources. There is no doubt that Lilly's key strength is in leading teams and individuals. The area in which she feels least confident is in variance analysis, which is part of managing finance and resources. She is aware of this, and so is the senior management team (SMT).

TASK

In your view, should Lilly's available time be focused on playing to her strengths, using her ability to relate to and inspire others in the interests of promoting the college's vision, or should that time be spent in attempting to perfect her grasp of variance analysis? What reasons would you give to support your argument?

DISCUSSION

On the face of it, 'fixing' the parts of our performance which are not quite up to scratch seems a very logical response to our personal development obligations. But, quite apart from begging the question of whether the particular behaviour can be learned, the 'plugging the gaps' approach may arguably yield fewer benefits than building on areas of existing competence. Despite his view that leaders can be made, Drucker is clear about the futility of wasting too much effort on trying to improve areas of low competence, (Drucker, 2001). Furthermore, we have to ask ourselves if just being 'competent' is what we are ultimately aiming for. Of course it makes sense to have a standard of achievement for leaders, just as it does for our students, but arguably this must, by definition, be a minimum standard. Surely a part of what we aim to do for learners – and let us include ourselves in this – is to offer the possibility of 'stretching' one's capabilities, taking natural strengths and using these to perform outstandingly in certain activities.

A view of leadership that is willing to accommodate the huge diversity of individual approaches, values and preferences may incline us to focus more on an individual's real strengths as a leader, and to appreciate the potential benefits of making the role fit the person rather than the other way around. But crucially, it also legitimises the acknowledgement of weaknesses, of which more later.

Common sense

Another criticism aimed at the blanket acceptance of competencies in leadership development is that they can lead to an emphasis on technical skills at the expense of relationship-building. The danger is that, in our desire to 'scientifically' evaluate and isolate the skill components of leadership, we somehow forget what years of experience, personal instinct and common sense have taught us. Research by Manchester Business School with shop-floor workers in manufacturing highlighted three key elements of successful people management:

- respect;
- recognition;
- relationships. (Pass, 2004)

What seemed to matter to these followers more than the behavioural minutiae of many competency frameworks was a few simple aspects of the way they were treated (being thanked for a job well done, observing social courtesies, being treated with respect, and a bit of 'give and take'). Again, this is consistent with the LSDA (2003) findings. None of this would have surprised the average, decent first-line manager fifty years ago.

In 2005, a letter in *People Management*, the professional journal for human resources specialists, argued strongly for a common-sense approach to leadership. Key themes here were:

- successful leaders lead others in the way *they* wish to be led;
- they communicate clear *objectives*;
- they *involve* people in planning and problem-solving;
- they agree *realistic* targets for team members to achieve;
- they give *support* and monitor progress of teams/individuals;
- they don't get over-involved in task, at the expense of *evaluating and improving performance*. (Pounder, 2005).

While these two perspectives – the P*eople Management* letter and the Manchester Business School research – have resulted in yet another form of recipe, they at least have the virtue of being relatively straightforward and unrestrictive. The lesson here seems to be that, however much we support the idea of competencies, we must ensure that they focus on a core of genuinely common success factors and do not ignore what centuries of experience of human relationships have taught us.

Classical perfection

Ironically, whether we adopt a competency approach to leadership development, or whether we subscribe to the view that leaders are either partly or wholly forged by innate qualities, natural flair and the 'right' set of personality characteristics, we are equally in danger of arriving at the same dead end. That is a seemingly unattainable ideal of leadership perfection, more akin to the heroes of ancient mythology than the realities of modern organisational life. The charismatic, larger-than-life, heroic leaders who populate so many of the 'How I did it' books on management best-seller lists may be inspiring, but are they helpful to those ordinary mortals like us trying to do a better job of leading their teams? All too often, their recipes for success disguise a reign based more on the cult of personality than on easily replicable behaviours. But, in just the same way, if we build detailed and all-encompassing competency structures to delineate how we want leaders to perform, we are equally at risk of implying that leadership success comes only from the ability to 'tick all the boxes'. Only those who wear their underpants on the outside need apply. We are back to poor old Graham whom we met at the beginning of this chapter.

DISCUSSION

Surely one of the characteristics of great leaders is their skill at surrounding themselves with people who compensate for the weaknesses that they have openly recognised in themselves? Some now feel that there is a clear case for leaders revealing their weaknesses, whether it be an eccentric approach to organising their time or a tendency to let their enthusiasm bulldoze every other opinion in its path. Revealing our weaknesses shows that we are human, imperfect and approachable (Goffee and Jones, 2000). This is partly what lies behind some of the recent focus on 'collaborative' leadership, which may be seen as a means of reconciling the ideal of leadership perfection with individual weaknesses. If we seek to compensate for imperfections in our own leadership by creating balance within the team, it may be possible to have 'the best of both worlds'.

So what question should we be asking?

We began this chapter by suggesting that the 'born or made' question is the wrong one to be asking. Perhaps the really important question is:

> *Should we subscribe to any single ideal model, or must we embrace a concept of leadership that makes room for individual styles, personalities, intuition, weaknesses and an incomplete 'toolkit' of behaviours?*

Rather than ask ourselves which of the thousands of recipes is the right one, we should perhaps consider this very diversity of answers to be a reflection of the variety of leadership styles which can all be effective, for different people, in different circumstances. The advantage of this mindset is that we can stop giving ourselves such a hard time for not living up to the model of perfection contained in the literature or training programme, and we can start developing an approach to leadership which works for us. The downside, on the other hand, is that suddenly someone has taken away the instruction booklet, and we are staring blankly at our strategic objectives as if they were a new DVD recorder. **In this view of the world, a leader's self-knowledge, and their ability to learn continuously and adapt will be the most critical attributes of all.**

Summary

So, we might summarise the pros and cons of the competency framework approach to leadership as follows.

Pros	Cons
Clarity	Comprehensive = too prescriptive
Consistency	Encourages 'cloning'
Accessibility	Obscures common sense
Professionalisation	Aspires to classical perfection
Non-alignment with born or made	

A lot of well-researched work has gone into developing leadership standards and qualities for the sector. It is not the intention here to undermine their usefulness as a tool for analysing performance and targeting development activity. What is legitimate, however, is to point out the risks inherent in an over-formulaic approach to one's own development as a leader, and the potential benefits of knowing yourself, understanding your real strengths and building a leadership approach around them. Undoubtedly, there are certain things that we have to be able to do to a reasonable standard in order to fulfil a leadership role, at whatever level. For this reason, we will refer to the leadership and management standards where helpful and appropriate. But we see no benefit in providing a further level of detail to what is already a pretty extensive set of guidelines. We believe it might be more stimulating to use our own research and experience to also look behind the standards at what seems to make the difference between competence and excellence in leadership.

The challenge then, and one we intend to address in the chapters that follow, is:

- how do we continue to improve our leadership performance in a way that is optimal for us and consistent with our own personality and values?
- how do we make use of the massive body of existing leadership knowledge, the National Standards and downright common sense to improve the way we lead while remaining true to ourselves and allowing for our imperfections?

Chapters 2–8

Over the course of the next seven chapters we will be examining what for us are the key themes associated with excellent leadership in the post-compulsory sector. Together, these themes form a useful framework for understanding your own strengths and values, your leadership 'brand', and for managing your development as a leader in a way that is consistent with that self-image, those values and your own personality.

Chapters 9–10

All of these themes are closely interlinked, to the extent that even separating them into chapters feels faintly artificial, so in the final two chapters of the book we will be addressing the importance of an integrated approach with our discussion of 'flexibility in leading change' and 'joined-up leadership'.

Leadership: an ethical dimension

Running through all of these themes is the idea of a set of professional ethics, or what Bennis and Thomas call a 'moral compass' (Bennis and Thomas, 2002). This is an underlying sense of right and wrong, a set of personal values, not necessarily explicit or sometimes even conscious, but strongly held nonetheless by excellent leaders. It regulates the way in which leaders apply the behaviours, skills and attitudes contained in these leadership themes. It cannot be enforced through procedures, which only tend to tell us how to act more efficiently (Drucker, 2001). It is a matter of judgement. When this 'compass' is working well, it ensures that decisions and actions are taken in the best interests of all stakeholders in the institution: staff, students, employers and so on. When it is not working well, then potentially positive behaviours and attributes can tip over into a 'dark side' of cynical, unethical and even illegal practices. In recent years, events in large corporations around the world have focused attention on this ethical dimension. Just within the post-compulsory sector, the years immediately following incorporation held some salutary lessons in how quickly commercial pressures could lead to dubious decision-making and financial mismanagement.

So under each of our themes we will be pointing out this 'dark side', partly to illustrate the impact that a well-calibrated 'moral compass' can have, but also to give readers an 'early-warning system' by which to recognise where their own decisions or behaviour may be straying from the straight and narrow.

2. Connecting with people

Introduction

We will begin our exploration of leadership themes by looking at how leaders 'connect' with people, because the way in which we relate to others has an impact on all of the other themes we will be discussing. When we talk about connecting with people we are referring to those things we do that build a productive relationship with others, the sort of relationship that means they are willing to be influenced and led by us. Obviously, this has links with other aspects of leadership, such as vision and values, motivation and taking decisive action, all of which we discuss in subsequent chapters. But here our focus is specifically on the personal interaction between leaders and their teams.

Our conversations with leaders in FE colleges confirmed the LSDA findings (Lumby et al., 2005) that productive relationships with peers, bosses and those you lead are central to leadership at all levels. So important is it that emotional intelligence and sensitivity in managing others was viewed in some quarters as the development *priority* for managers in the lifelong learning sector.

So in this chapter we shall be attempting to answer some of the more complex and problematic questions about leadership, the answers to which lie deeper than management techniques and recipes.

● What gives leaders credibility?

● What makes us warm to some people and not others?

● How is it that some people influence our thoughts and actions, while others we dismiss?

- Is it just about interpersonal skills?
- What really makes us happy to be led by someone?
- How do we identify leaders who do this well?
- What if a leader 'connects', but for the wrong reasons?
- How can we develop our leadership practice in this area?

Why connecting with people is so important

Sir Peter Parker, ex-Chairman of British Rail and the British Institute of Management, saw this quality in Lord Mountbatten, referring to the *immense trouble* he took to *connect with the people*, (Parker, 1996, p33).

Why is this so important? Well, our effectiveness as leaders is determined by our followers' willingness to deploy *discretionary effort* (Yankelovich and Associates, 1983; Immerwahr, 1983), in other words to go that 'extra mile'. Research suggests that people choose to contribute to the full potential of their ability, energy and creativity, based partly on how they are treated by the organisation. Indeed, research by Bath University's Work and Employment Research Centre suggests that the biggest influence on employee commitment is their relationship with their immediate manager (Hutchinson et al., 2003). We can all think of examples where people choose to do no more than the minimum. This is their choice, but it is largely our behaviour towards them, as leaders, which determines that choice. Of course, to call it a choice implies that this is something entirely susceptible to rational thought, and yet we know it is just as much an emotional response that makes us willing to be led by someone. *Encouraging the heart* is key to effective leadership and to do this we must *harness emotions* as well as logical argument (Hooper and Potter, 2000; Kouzes and Posner, 1995).

Accepting that most of our organisations could probably improve the extent to which their leaders engage and connect with staff, what should be their prime focus of attention? Every organisation wants leaders who have **credibility** and **influence**. But how do we achieve this? It is tempting to focus in on communications and interpersonal skills, not least because they are a relatively easy-to-diagnose training need. If we do not communicate with our team members it is hard to see how we are going to establish productive relationships with them. Worse than this, in the absence of clear information about what is going on and how they can play their part, people will tend to assume that something is being hidden from them. Actually, it is even worse than that, because, having assumed that you are hiding something from them, they then go on to make up what it is you are hiding and, before you know it, this has become the new organisational reality.

Openness comes high on most people's list of what makes them follow others. For leaders this means **sharing information**, whether or not you feel people are fascinated by all of it, simply because it reassures them that it is available to them. It means being as frank about bad news as we are about the good, because people will be more inclined then to believe us when we have something positive to say. This can be tough for leaders who worry about 'frightening the horses'. But we can still be supportive as leaders while helping people confront what Jim Collins calls the *brutal facts* (Collins, 2001). Staff are wary of change but more likely to trust the boss who explains why the change is needed. (More of this in Chapter 8, when we talk about how leaders respond to setbacks.)

OK, so simply communicating with people in the first place is a good start. But the *way* in which leaders actually handle set-piece presentations, team talks, meetings and individual interviews will *also* have a profound impact on their authority, credibility and how well respected they are. Handle such interactions in a clumsy or insensitive fashion and productive relationships will be severely undermined.

So there we have it. Send everyone on a communications and interpersonal skills course. Well, not quite. Consider the correlation between expertise in these techniques and the engagement of staff. Is it really positive and linear? Or once a reasonable level of aptitude has been reached does the law of diminishing returns begin to apply? In fact, is our response to highly slick speakers and perfectly rehearsed delivery just as likely to be a sceptical search for the catch? In other words, important though these interpersonal skills are, might we argue that they are equivalent to Herzberg's hygiene factors when it comes to connecting with people – something that only prevents people from being dissatisfied (Herzberg, 1966)? In other words, leaders need to master a certain level of competence in communication and interpersonal skills so as not to demotivate those they lead, but beyond that, it is other factors that really build productive relationships.

The exception to this, significantly, may be *listening*. We are less likely to distrust someone who listens to us more expertly than someone who talks to us more expertly. Listening well is one of the most effective ways of building rapport with those we lead, and probably one of the most underutilised by managers. When was the last time someone really listened empathetically to you, and how did it make you feel about them? And when was the last time your institution sent someone on a listening course?

We have no intention of covering interpersonal techniques here, partly for reasons of space, but also because there are better sources of this and many readers may already be familiar with the material. No, we are more concerned here with those other factors we mentioned. But first, let us drop in on a meeting between Sean, a section head, and Tucker, one of his team. They are discussing a classroom observation.

TASK

Read the following exchange and try to identify what Sean is doing right. (This is always good leadership practice, but may be strangely unfamiliar to some leaders you know!) Did the exchange go as well as it could have? Why do you think this is?

Sean   *Come in, Tucker, and have a seat. I thought we could use the meeting room for this chat, as it gives us a bit more privacy.*

Tucker   *Thanks, mate. So, how's things with you?*

Sean   *Well, I thought we'd talk about the classroom observation I did of your NVQ Level 3 group yesterday. I'm going to run through what I thought you did well, and then we can talk about how you could potentially make things even better, and really impress the OFSTED inspectors. A personal mention next month would be a feather in your cap, eh?*

Tucker   *Be quite a feather in your cap too, boss, wouldn't it? The holiday was great, by the way. Thanks for asking.*

Sean   *Well, you know, I see this team as like an upside-down triangle. I'm just here to support you guys, and help you do your job to the best of your ability.*

Tucker   *Is that what you're doing on all those working parties, when we don't see hide nor hair of you for days on end? Talking us up to the powers that be, eh? Well that's a relief.*

Sean   *Hey, I'm allowed to learn and develop too, you know.*

Tucker   *Still, the section did get a bit caned in the last report, didn't it? And, as the new boy in charge, you'd just love an early goal.*

Sean   *Well, we're not there yet, and you need to address a few issues before we share in any glory.*

Tucker   *What the hell is that supposed to mean?*

Sean   *Well . . . er . . . let me say, first of all, that the content of the session came over as well-researched and presented in a really entertaining and accessible way. I thought your control of discipline and the way you dealt with the couple of disruptive girls was an object lesson in classroom management. Well done!*

Tucker   *Thanks. But?*

Sean   *Oh, come on! That's all really positive stuff. You should feel really pleased with yourself.*

Tucker   *What makes you think I don't?*

DISCUSSION

Well, it is fair to say that did not perhaps go quite as Sean had planned. Is this simply down to Tucker being a fully paid-up member of the awkward squad? What went wrong? After all, Sean had taken the trouble to communicate with Tucker in the first place. We can safely assume that he intended to be open about what he commended in Tucker's classroom performance and what he felt needed further improvement. Furthermore, Sean had taken care to be professional in his approach. He was prepared. He had picked a suitable environment for the feedback. He made it clear what he wanted to talk about and how he would structure the discussion. He tried to give some positive feedback first, with specific examples. He even adopted a pretty friendly, informal tone. Despite all of this, however, as you have doubtless already concluded, he was dead before Tucker walked into the room.

What was missing from this conversation was trust, and that cannot be summoned up in the space of one meeting. Why did Tucker have so little trust in his section leader? Their conversation reveals three factors.

Courtesy	Sean ploughed straight into his spiel, without taking the time to observe any of the common social courtesies, such as asking how Tucker was or how his holiday went. If this is par for the course, how much does he care about his team?
Honesty	Sean's view on leadership and his taking the trouble to identify a positive incentive for Tucker were admirable, but why not be straight about how a good inspection would reflect well on them both?
Visibility	If the only context in which your team sees you is formal meetings, how can you build the rapport which trust is based on, or learn enough about them to treat them like fellow human beings? (See Courtesy.)

So, good communications and interpersonal skills alone, however well-polished, do not result in credibility and influence as a leader. Clearly, there has to be a degree of trust and respect as well. We will go on to look in more detail at issues such as courtesy, honesty and visibility, as well as discussing what else builds trust between leaders and teams. But first, let us begin to summarise some of these points in a simple diagram (see Figure 2.1).

Do the people you lead, as well as your colleagues and your boss, trust and respect you? We might all be inclined to answer yes to this question, although independent research by MORI has indicated that only 28 per cent of people would trust business leaders to tell the truth. While this is an improvement on politicians and journalists (both 18 per cent), it should still give senior managers in post-compulsory education (PCE) pause for thought (MORI, 2003). And even if we think we are trusted, how strong do we think this is on, say, a scale of 1 (as far as I could throw you) to 10 (I implicitly take every word you say as gospel)?

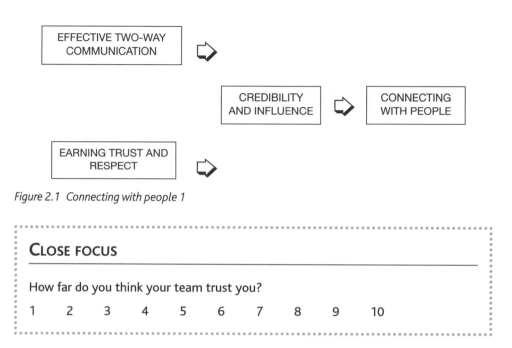

Figure 2.1 Connecting with people 1

CLOSE FOCUS

How far do you think your team trust you?

| 1 | 2 | 3 | 4 | 5 | 6 | 7 | 8 | 9 | 10 |

One might argue that because colleges, like many organisations, are inherently competitive environments comprised of able and ambitious professionals looking for development and promotion then it is always going to be difficult to build trust (Kets de Vries, 2005). However, this should not prevent us from trying, and the level of competitiveness versus collaboration in the culture is, after all, something leaders can play a part in determining.

Bass and Avolio (1994) describe the four components which differentiate transformational leadership from the merely transactional as the four Is:

- inspirational motivation;
- intellectual stimulation;
- individualised consideration;
- idealised influence.

The first three concern providing meaning and challenge, encouraging creativity, and attending to individual growth and development, but the last, Idealised influence, is all about respect, trust and acting with integrity.

So what is it about the way we behave as leaders that builds mutual trust and respect and thereby our ability to influence others?

Here we start to move away from the realm of traditional interpersonal skills, which imply a rather instrumental approach to human relationships, and towards the notion of emotional intelligence, which sees successful relationships as rooted in self-awareness and sensitivity to the emotions of others. The four components described by Goleman et al. (2002) are:

- self-awareness – knowing your strengths and weaknesses, having a sense of your own worth, being aware of your own emotions;
- self-management – control of your own emotions, honesty, integrity, flexibility;
- social awareness – recognising the emotions and needs of others;
- relationship management – collaborating effectively, handling conflict, influencing others.

Let us break this down a bit and consider what it means for our behaviour as leaders.

Honesty, authenticity and integrity

Openness is closely linked with *honesty, authenticity and integrity*. We can only judge our leaders' words by comparing them with their body language, their actions and what they achieve. Trust is reinforced by *doing what you say you will do*, but also by *being yourself*. The most successful leaders demonstrate congruence, a comfortable fit between their personality and their leadership style, their words and their actions, their actions and their own personal values (Kouzes and Posner, 1995) – see Figure 2.2.

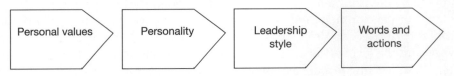

Figure 2.2 *Authenticity and consistency*

So, if everyone is watching you so closely, how do you manage to hide all your faults and weaknesses? Maybe you don't. Simply ask yourself which is more likely to build rapport, a person who reveals their weaknesses or a person who pretends to have none? Disclosure, being honest about ourselves and our vulnerabilities, is known to help build trust and rapport because it establishes common ground. We are all just human after all. Showing that, as a leader, demonstrates empathy. It also helps people to see where they can help you, and so encourages teamwork (Goffee and Jones, 2000).

Visibility and approachability

Openness stems also from a leader's *approachability and visibility*. Trust requires familiarity (Luhmann, 1979). People find it hard to trust leaders they never see, and having an 'open door' will not result in you being more visible, however much the less affiliative and sociable leaders among us may try to convince themselves otherwise. Visibility and open, honest communication require going out into the organisation and *listening to people*, as well as talking with them. This means investing time, not in accounts, reports, strategic plans, curriculum proposals, etc., but in just listening to people. It is significant that, in this era of high-speed communications, some institutions have actually implemented e-mail-free days to slow the growth of a 'memo' culture and encourage people to actually talk to each other.

It is said that Napoleon's downfall began when he stopped explaining his plans to his troops, sleeping on the battleground with his soldiers and being straightforward about potential difficulties as well as rewards. After Austerlitz, he was less inclined to deal with generals directly and introduced more distance and formality into his leadership style (Kim et al., 2002). Your own leadership ambitions may fall some way short of conquering Europe, but the same principle applies.

Fairness and decency

Approachability and distance are a tricky balance. We know that once we are given leadership responsibility, we can no longer be just one of the team. There may be situations that require us to think and act objectively and dispassionately. Another way we earn our team's trust and respect is by treating them with *fairness and decency*, and being seen to be consistently impartial in dealing with people and performance. But too much distance between a leader and the team hinders open communication, inhibits trust and prevents us from sensing situations that require our intervention (Goffee and Jones, 2000). Decency also means observing the common courtesies, such as greeting people, thanking them for their efforts and asking after their welfare: small, but important details that the distant leader can neglect.

Demonstrating trust and respect

So far we have been looking at how we *earn* our team's trust and respect. But this is a two-way street. People are less inclined to respect and trust those who clearly do not respect and trust them, (Luhmann, 1979). So we must also consider how, as leaders, we demonstrate our trust and respect towards those we lead. Remember the Manchester Business School research we referred to in Chapter 1? The three Rs: Respect, Recognition and Relationships (Pass, 2004).

TASK

Pause for a moment here and jot down half a dozen ways in which you, as a leader, demonstrate trust and respect towards your team. Then compare your list with what we have covered below.

DISCUSSION

- *Sharing information.* One area we have touched upon already and that is communication. Not communicating your plans and ideas sends a strong signal that you do not trust those around you. They do not have your respect.

- *Giving people responsibility.* We can also show our respect and trust by giving people responsibility, then 'setting them free' to get on with what they are good at (Wells, 1996). Empowerment, an overused term, indicates a leader's trust and respect for team members, so long as it is matched by responsibility and competence on the team member's part and support from the team leader. Good leaders increase people's freedom in line with their competence and record of delivery (Hooper and Potter, 2000).

- *Caring.* This may seem an incongruous term amid the cut and thrust of most commercial organisations, but may be more readily understood by educational institutions with a tradition of pastoral care. Simply *caring* about the people in our team is a mark of respect. This does not mean wrapping them in cotton wool or indulging in corporate group hugs, but simply *attaching the same importance to the relationships* as you do to the task. Checking up on how they feel, what has been going on in their lives, whether they are happy in their work, shows respect because it treats them like human beings, not resources. Remember Sean and his inattention to the social courtesies? Well, this is all part of being interested in your people as individuals, not just as a way of delivering objectives. This is almost impossible to fake, because people can sense very well whether or not you care about them. It is arguably, therefore, not easy to learn. However, taking the trouble to get to know people is probably a good start.

- *Space for informal, social contact.* While we are on the subject of caring, what about the social dimension? We are not all thrilled by the idea of work-based social events. Some people like to keep work and leisure very separate. They are not interested in spending time socially with colleagues, still less with bosses. So knowing how your team members feel about this is important. But that does not mean we should lose sight of the idea that work can be enjoyed, that, given the right environment, people can have fun at work and may be all the better for it. However you choose to do it, leaders who make space for a little informality, humour and social interaction, as well as the task, tend to have better-motivated teams.

So, earning and demonstrating trust and respect is a hugely complex and multidimensional process. Perhaps it might help to summarise what we have said so far by adding to our earlier diagram (see Figure 2.3).

At this point, you might well be thinking, 'Hang on, so why did I spend all those years studying to become competent in my chosen profession if my team's respect is based purely on all these things? Whatever happened to a love of teaching and learning?'

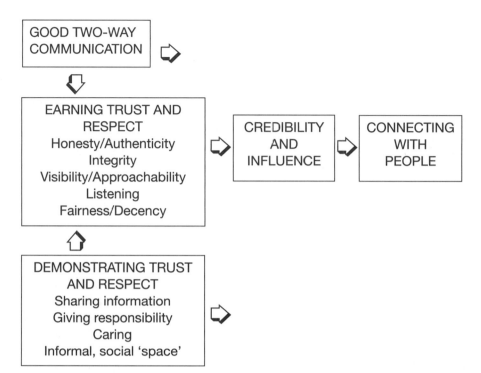

Figure 2.3 Connecting with people 2

Competence and expertise

It is a fair question, and undoubtedly we can respect those whose skills and knowledge we admire or whose expertise we aspire to. Our trust in the surgeon operating on us might be well be undermined if we notice her reading our chart upside down. So how might this apply to leadership?

CLOSE FOCUS

Look again at the discussion between Sean and Tucker. We are given no clue here as to what Sean's level of professional expertise as a teacher is. But what difference do you think it would have made to the relationship if:

1. Sean's expertise had been at a lower level in comparison to Tucker's?

2. It had been demonstrably superior to Tucker's level of expertise?

How important is this in comparison to the other issues they have?

And finally, what if this were a head of school and section leader discussing budget performance, not a classroom observation?

It is fair to argue that you can lead a team successfully without being able to do the jobs of everyone in it. But is that simply because at more senior levels, where this becomes inevitable, one is judged on one's skills as a manager and leader, not a teacher, or marketer or accountant? Many readers of this book will have been experts in their chosen trade or profession before entering teaching. Once in education, what is more important – remaining one of the best engineers/hair stylists/car mechanics around, or becoming a great teacher?

Whatever our views on these questions, what we can agree on is that people respect expertise in their leaders. What sort of expertise is most influential depends on circumstances and understanding your own expertise, your strengths and limitations, is fundamental to being an honest and authentic leader. The real catalyst in all this, however, is your *attitude* to what you do. A highly expert but bored and weary leader is pretty much like a highly gifted but bored and weary teacher. Neither inspire us to do our best.

Enthusiasm, conviction, passion

If we think about leaders who have connected with us in a way that was motivating and energising, part of their influence will probably have stemmed from their own enthusiasm for what they were doing and what the team was trying to achieve. There are close links here, again, with later themes, such as vision and storytelling, but there is also a strong connection with honesty and authenticity. Fake passion, like fake caring, can be spotted a mile away. So, as a leader, it is important to think carefully about what you value and believe in, so that the conviction you display when talking with people is genuine.

We can now complete our simple diagram as in Figure 2.4.

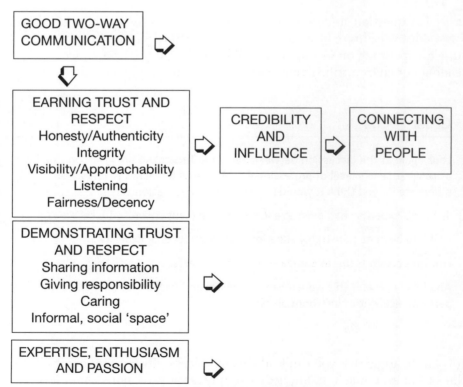

Figure 2.4 Connecting with people 3

TASK

Let us now take a look at another conversation between Winston, the facilities manager, and Mo, campus car park attendant. Read through it, then compare it to the example earlier between Sean and Tucker. What are the differences? Which leader would you rather work for?

Winston — *Mo, sorry to chase after you like that. I'm running late for a meeting, but I spotted you there and couldn't let the opportunity pass to have a quick word.*

Mo — *Well, I'm on my break. I was just off to get some lunch.*

Winston — *Oh dear, I'm so sorry. Look I know you've been having a hard time of it lately with your son and everything, but we really do need to talk. Let's just pop in the canteen here. We'll grab a quiet corner and I'll get you a sandwich. (They do this and sit down.)*

So, how are things at home, Mo?

Mo — *Alright, I suppose. The police haven't come back yet about whether they're going to charge him or not . . .*

Winston — *You're still on tenterhooks then? You must be feeling worried sick. Look if there's anything I can do, you know, in terms of arranging some time off or anything . . .*

Mo — *Thanks, but that's OK. There's nothing I can do at home at the moment . . . Look I don't want to be rude, but what's this about?*

Winston — *I'm not going to beat around the bush, Mo, I've had complaints about you getting shirty with staff and visitors.*

Mo — *Oh have you? It wouldn't be that idiot Head of Business and whatever, would it? He's always parking wherever he likes.*

Winston — *I can't tell you that, Mo, and it wouldn't help. You're a good guy and loyal employee who happens to be going through a rough patch at home. I realise you do a bit of a thankless job, and generally I'm happy to back you up. But I can't have you shouting and bawling at staff, let alone visitors. So what are we going to do?*

Mo — *It's not my fault. No bugger will make a decision about the patch of ground behind the Engineering block. Everyone thinks they can park on it, and then I get a rollocking when the minibus can't get out.*

Winston — *OK, that's my fault, Mo. I was supposed to clear it at the last health and safety meeting and . . . well, you know what my memory's like. Tell me what you think is the best option. If we can agree I promise to clear that with people today. Will you then promise me no more hissy fits?*

Mo — *Well . . .*

DISCUSSION

What were your thoughts? This wasn't quite as polished a performance by Winston in terms of organising a proper interview, introducing the issue or checking his part in the problem. However, how would you rate Winston's emotional intelligence compared to Sean's?

Here is a leader who seems to care about his staff, understands what makes them tick, admits his own faults and weaknesses, and is straightforward about what he wants.

The 'dark side'

So, is the ability to connect with people a universally positive thing? Well, as we suggested at the start of this chapter, like all leadership behaviour, it must be tempered by some sense of ethical or moral direction. It is not too difficult to foresee the consequences of a faulty 'moral compass' here. Whatever we say about authenticity and honesty, history has shown that a morally flawed leader can believe passionately in the course he is taking and, given the ability to tap into people's emotions, fears and prejudices, can mobilise an entire nation into calamitous acts of inhumanity. But equally, on a smaller scale, leaders in organisations can fall into the trap of abusing the trust and credibility that they have earned. Persuasion becomes bullying and manipulation, objectivity becomes isolation, and the good of the team or college is replaced by more personal goals and ambitions. To guard against this, we must, as leaders, be prepared to ask ourselves some tough questions.

● In whose interests am I acting here?
● Have I been open about my agenda?
● How would I feel if I were in this person's shoes?
● What is my real objective, and how does this fit with my values and those of the organisation?

Earlier we eavesdropped on Sean and Tucker. We might suppose that Sean's motives were entirely honourable, even if his leadership was somewhat inept. But what if this antagonising of Tucker had been deliberate, disguised behind a procedurally correct and professionally managed interchange but intended to provoke Tucker into behaviour which Sean could legitimately use as a lever to get rid of him?

Issues for the Lifelong Learning sector

This examination of the 'dark side' of influence in relationships echoes some of the debate within the sector around managerialism and the dangers of applying management processes and techniques to what some would regard as communities of dedicated and mutually supportive professionals (Jameson, 2006). Are open debate and consensus being replaced by management control and the more or less subtle tools of workforce persuasion that some associate with big corporate institutions? Have the changes in the sector resulted in a culture where performance improvement becomes a matter of well-executed 'interpersonal encounters' and clever manipulation, and not a shared desire to learn and improve?

CLOSE FOCUS

In your own experience, are concerns about creeping managerialism in the lifelong learning sector well-founded? Given what you have read in this chapter, what might be the challenges in aspiring to greater levels of emotional intelligence, mutual trust and respect, and ethical leadership while pursuing an increasingly commercial agenda?

Self-evaluation and development

Now we turn to how your own brand of leadership might reflect this theme of connecting with people. Is this a real strength for you, or is it a part of your leadership portfolio which might never be your strongest suit, but around which you can develop strategies to ensure it is not a damaging influence on your relationships with your team and your colleagues?

How might we evaluate ourselves against this aspect of leadership? Psychometric tests, in particular personality questionnaires, providing they are reputable and expertly administered, may give you some clues. They may reveal whether you are, by nature, someone who seeks and enjoys company, someone who likes to influence and sell ideas, someone who is motivated to care about and nurture others. But what does your own experience tell you? (You may have to be brutally honest here.) Are you the sort of person whom people naturally warm to, who establishes rapport and empathy instinctively and easily with strangers? When at work, is your tendency to channel all your focus into getting the task completed, or checking up on how the team are feeling and ensuring they are happy?

Look again at the four aspects of emotional intelligence. How good are you at recognising emotions in others, sensing how they are feeling? How well do you control your own emotions under pressure? How do you respond to conflict with other people?

You can use feedback from your boss, colleagues and people in your team, whether informally, or through more formal processes. This is often referred to as 360-degree feedback. Used properly, and accompanied by coaching and support, this is known to help improve leadership skills (Conger, 2004). Equally you might ask close friends and family. All this will help you address the first of those emotional intelligence factors, self-awareness, and that, in itself, will help you manage relationships with others better.

If this area is a strength for you, then you can build on it further. Look for more senior role models with whom you share this talent and observe what they do. You might want to think about projects or secondments that take you out of your 'comfort zone' and require you to influence people over whom you have no formal authority. Perhaps there are environments, such as external forums, where your influencing skills can be stretched and put to good use for your organisation. Why not volunteer for one of these? Become a mentor to new and developing managers in your institution. Your relationship skills will help you coach others and you will undoubtedly learn more about yourself from them.

But what if connecting with people is not your natural strong suit? Well, first of all, do not try to change who you are and be Captain Charisma. The result is likely to be excruciating. Focus instead on aspects of behaviour covered in this chapter that are not skills or personality dependent. We can all ensure that we are being as open and honest as we can with our team. We can all try to share information more and keep our promises, and we can all treat people fairly and decently. Asking after people's welfare and thanking them for a job well done is more a matter of effort than superb social skills, and the same may be said for going out and listening to people. You might find it more of an effort, and feel more uncomfortable doing it than a natural 'people person' would, but your efforts will be appreciated all the more for that by your team.

Of course, there are interpersonal skills training programmes, and you may find these useful, particularly if you need to acquire basic competence in 'procedural' exchanges, but most leaders, and certainly the FE leaders we spoke to, ascribe most of their learning in this area to structured experience and positive role models rather than formal education and training. The message here is get out and experiment with new behaviour, and do not be afraid to ask for feedback.

Summary of key points

In this chapter we have studied how connecting with people stems from having credibility and influence as a leader, and that this, in turn, is enhanced by:

- good two-way communications;
- emotional intelligence;
- earning and demonstrating trust and respect;
- having expertise in one's role, but also a passion and enthusiasm for what you and the team are doing.

3. Instinct for opportunity

Introduction

One of the key words for the Lifelong Learning sector in the twenty-first century is responsiveness. We are urged to be responsive to local and national training needs, and the quality of our performance and provision is evaluated, in part, in terms of our responsiveness. But the responsiveness of any organisation depends upon the readiness of its leaders – at all levels – to 'read' and respond to emerging needs in the local environment and trends and patterns that are developing at a national level, too. This chapter looks at the leader's role in identifying opportunities for their organisation in general and for their team in particular. It is an aspect of the leader's role which can act as a positive counterbalance to the daily imperatives of externally imposed goals and systems of accountability. It is an area of the job which calls upon you to exercise your ingenuity, your imagination, your entrepreneurial skills and your lateral thinking. It can also demand a high level of skill in researching and interpreting data, in diplomacy and deal-making, and – above all – in communication. The National Occupational Standards present this area of practice as consisting of activities such as:

- identifying and interpreting relevant key issues;
- gathering appropriate information;
- conducting logical analyses.

Listed in this way, these may well not have you jumping up and down with excitement. But when you consider that these very same priorities wouldn't look amiss if included in an operational briefing for James Bond, you may begin to recognise the potential for interesting and challenging – and ultimately rewarding – activity.

Interpreting the environment

A theme that recurred time and time again in our conversations with leaders in FE was the importance of knowing when and how to respond to changes in the environment in which the organisation operates. This was about consciously anticipating shifting needs and trends, about constantly monitoring what was happening politically and socially, but also about using one's instincts, one's 'gut-feel' for potential opportunities in provision, continuously 'scanning' the environment and taking a risk now and then. An essential aspect of our continuing professional development is that we have a responsibility to keep ourselves abreast of local and national issues which are relevant to our role and purpose within the organisation. This is true for all professionals working in the Lifelong Learning sector, but particularly for those in a leadership role. To lead a team effectively, the leader must have a clear idea of which way they are going and why. This will be broadly dictated by the purpose and vision of the organisation but, within those parameters, there will be opportunities for innovation and initiative. We can express this formula for responsiveness as follows:

> purpose and vision + alertness to environment = responsive provision
> (organisational level) (team leader level)

Let's have a look at some examples of this 'environmental alertness' and how it contributes to the responsive organisation.

TASK

As you read through the scenario which follows, consider these questions:

- What information did Orson need to have in order to formulate his plan?

- Where and how is he most likely to have come by that information?

- What does this tell us about Orson's professional development activities?

You can compare your answers to our discussion at the end of this section.

Scenario 1

Orson is Head of School of Business. He has a strong team which includes people with substantial experience of the world of business and commerce, people with higher degrees in business or related subjects, and people who have both of these. Two local schools have begun offering Business Studies at AS and A level, and some of Orson's team have expressed worries about this in terms of competition and the future of their own jobs. Orson, however, with his instinct for opportunity, has envisioned a way to turn this situation to the advantage of his team and the college as a whole. He takes his idea to his Head of Faculty, Jean.

Jean	*A foundation degree in Business?*
Orson	*Absolutely! Why not? Look at what we've got going for us. A likely increase in the number of kids locally with a level three qualification in Business. Increasing numbers of 18-year-olds going on to higher ed. A growing trend for kids to do their degree while living at home – but we've got no local university . . .*
Jean	*Hang on. We'd have to have it validated, you know, do it in collaboration with a university. That won't be easy.*
Orson	*Yes, but having no local university not only means we'd be the only ones to offer these kids an 'at home' degree, it also means there's no one to see us as direct competitors. We could go to the nearest university – even that's miles away – and suggest to them that we run a foundation degree as part of a collaborative provision. And that would benefit everybody, because students would move on to them if they wanted to progress further. And the foundation degree would provide a progression route here, too, for our level three business students who wanted to go on to a degree . . .*
Jean	*But, Orson, do we have the capacity to do this? Aren't the team pretty overloaded as it is, without . . .*
Orson	*No, no. That's the beauty of it. My guess is that numbers entering for level three qualifications will level out now or even drop because of the new competition from these schools. So this is an ideal opportunity. And we need to get things rolling now. We really do. Because these things take time, and if numbers do drop and staff get reallocated as a consequence, we won't be in a position to take advantage of this opportunity.*
Jean	*OK, Orson. Do me a business plan and I'll take it to the SLT [Senior Leadership Team]. And hey – don't forget the projected costings.*

DISCUSSION

Orson had collected various pieces of data here which, *taken together,* gave him the inspiration and rationale for his proposal. We can set these out as in Table 3.1.

What is significant here – what makes Orson appear to have an instinct for opportunity – is not just that he knows what's happening institutionally, locally, regionally and nationally, but that he has *put all this data together and drawn some conclusions from the composite picture.* This is what we mean when we talk about having the ability to read a situation. It is about making connections between apparently disparate trends, seeing a potentially advantageous pattern where someone else, who provides themselves with less of an overview, may see only random developments.

Table 3.1 Collected data

WHAT HE'S AWARE OF	TYPE OF DATA	LIKELY SOURCE
Change of provision in two local schools	Local environment	Local paper School websites Network contacts
Growth of foundation degrees in FE colleges	National initiative	Education press White Papers Conferences
Likely increase in the number of local learners with a Level 3 qualification in Business	Local trend (projected)	Local paper School websites Network contacts Deductive reasoning
Increasing numbers of 18-year-olds going on to higher education	National trend	Education press DfES website Targets and circulars
Growing trend for undergraduates to live at home	National trend	Broadsheet press Education press
No local university	Local environment	Pretty hard to miss!
College can offer a collaborative rather than a competitive relationship with the university in question	Local environment Regional environment National trend	Deductive reasoning and strategic thinking
Numbers entering for Level 3 qualifications likely to level or drop	Local environment	Local paper School websites Network contacts Deductive reasoning
Timing is essential: a small window of opportunity	Local environment Organisational environment	College strategic plan Deductive reasoning

So what does all this suggest to us about Orson's professional development activities? Well, clearly he puts some effort into keeping himself up to date with policies, trends, publications and developments on all four essential levels:

● organisationally;
● locally;
● regionally;
● nationally.

At the end of this chapter we'll look at some tips for how you might be able to provide yourself with a similar ongoing overview within the time constraints of your demanding role.

People who excel at soaking up this kind of data about the world around them and accurately spotting which way the wind is blowing are vital to the success of Lifelong Learning organisations, given the increasingly competitive marketplace in which they are being asked to operate. In his book *The tipping point*, Malcolm Gladwell refers to them as 'mavens', from the Yiddish term for someone who collects information (Gladwell, 2000). And yet the leaders we spoke to were very clear that this is not just about rational analysis. It involves using one's instincts as well to determine what bits of information are truly significant and where the opportunity lies to experiment and take risks. Leaders are generally overloaded with data of one sort or another. Effective leaders can spot patterns and see the context for a decision, what Heifetz and Laurie call *getting on the balcony*, being able to 'see the wood for the trees' enables these leaders to challenge the status quo and thereby continuously learn from and adapt to their surroundings. This is what Bennis calls being a *first-class noticer* – the ability to anticipate and spot connections, to know what is relevant and what is not (Bennis, 2004; Heifetz and Laurie, 1997; Kouzes and Posner, 1995).

So this *instinct for opportunity* is not just about responsiveness to the marketplace, but also about responding to opportunities to learn and develop, both as individuals and as an organisation. FE principals we spoke to spent between 30 per cent and 50 per cent of their time focused on the world outside their college. At all levels leaders need to beware the temptation to get so wrapped up in the daily minutiae of their roles that they fail to hold their team, department or college up to the mirror of the outside world and question what they see. Ned Herrmann, developer of the *whole brain* model, refers to this as being *stuck in your own mental traffic jam* (Herrmann, 1996). He sees a need for creative leaders who not only challenge assumptions and see patterns and connections, but who are also opportunistic in seizing the chances these dynamic situations present to them.

TASK

Now read through this second scenario. Consider what it has in common with the first and where it differs. You may like to jot down some notes as you read so that you can compare your answers with what we have to say in the discussion at the scenario's end.

Scenario 2

Graham is head of section for English for Speakers of Other Languages (ESOL), leading a team of two full-time and three fractional lecturers. He is approaching retirement and has been thinking lately about the issues of succession and capacity. This train of thought has been triggered by the growing numbers of newly arrived immigrants from Eastern Europe who are settling in the town and its surrounding area. Graham believes that there is an urgent need for rapid growth in the provision of ESOL courses locally in order to improve the

▶

employment prospects and social integration of this growing population. He also believes that this is consistent with the college's vision of 'adapting to the developing needs of the community'. And so he decides to have a word with Lilly, his Head of School.

Lilly   You mean expand existing provision? That would mean taking on at least one more fractional lecturer.

Graham   You're missing the point. What I'm saying is that this could be enormous. I'm not talking about tinkering around with a few more part-time hours; I'm talking about an opportunity for us to get a TESOL teacher training programme up and running, and at the same time some outreach ESOL programmes out there in the community. There's a growing demand nationally for ESOL teachers, and our expanded provision would provide teaching practice placements . . .

Lilly   We've been told – all the Heads of School have been told – that we can't issue any more fractional contracts without direct approval from Finance.

Graham   I don't believe this. You're not listening to a word I say, are you? What have fractional contracts got to do with it? This is a huge opportunity. It would meet an urgent local need. It's bang in line with the college vision. It'd be self-sustaining in terms of finance and human resources . . .

Lilly   Look, I'm not discussing anything if you're going to shout.

Graham   (Heading for the door) Oh, forget it. Just forget it. I'll be retiring in a few months. Why should I care? Let some private outfit spot the opportunity and put this section out of business. Let's see how you like that.

DISCUSSION

Oh dear. It would be fair to say that Graham is demonstrating an equally acute instinct for opportunity as Orson. He, too, has evidently kept himself abreast of local and national trends and developments. He, too, has clearly demonstrated the ability to look at the accumulation of data and read in it a pattern which indicates an opportunity for the college to expand its provision while meeting local and national needs. We might even say he deserves some credit for sustaining his enthusiasm and professional development right up to his imminent retirement. So why do we have the feeling that this is one opportunity the college is going to let slip by?

What Graham illustrates here is that having an instinct for opportunity is not just about reading the political and social environment. It is also about reading people and situations. There is a strong connection here with the emotional intelligence that we talked about in Chapter 2. Influencing others is not just about having the correct data gathered and a compelling argument marshalled. It is about understanding other people's emotions and points of view, and recognising what kind of approach is most likely to meet with success. 'First-class noticers' do not just spot the opportunity to introduce new courses or market the organisation to a different target audience. They also read relationships accurately enough to see when to congratulate somebody, recognise their contribution, commiserate with them, or try to change their mind about something. Having a good idea is not enough if you do not choose how and when to present this opportunity to others with sufficient coherence, persuasiveness and determination.

The bottom line here is that Graham was irritable and impatient and that his Head of School was clearly not in the mood to listen properly to his proposals. They could both do with going away and reading Chapter 2 of this book because the problem lay not in the validity or otherwise of Graham's idea, but in the failure of both parties to exercise all those *connecting with people* skills. Furthermore, as Lilly's response demonstrates, potential opportunities can be all too easily stifled or ignored through inept leadership, and in this sense she should stand as a warning to us all. As Kanter (1984) points out, there is always a danger in leadership that it may appear unreceptive to innovation from below.

In both these scenarios we have seen the efforts of team leaders to communicate their reading of the situation, their identification of an opportunity, upwards to their line manager. The business of communicating such ideas in the other direction, from the leader to his or her team, will form part of the subject of the next chapter.

CLOSE FOCUS

We've used the expression in this chapter an instinct for opportunity. To what extent do you think this ability to identify opportunities really is an instinct that some possess and others don't?

DISCUSSION

This question really echoes very closely the 'born or made' debate and we would probably want to respond to it in exactly the same way. While some people may *appear* to have a 'nose' for the main chance and others apparently wouldn't see a good opportunity even if one fell on them, it would probably be equally true to say that the ability to spot a good opportunity comes as a result of being alert to what's going on in the relevant environment. And that 'environmental alertness' is achieved by:

- keeping scrupulously abreast of current developments;
- building and sustaining appropriate networks;
- carefully focused research.

Talk to anyone who has a name for being ahead of the game and you're likely to find that they work hard at all three of those activities.

The 'dark side'

So, at its best, this instinct for opportunity allows leaders in Lifelong Learning to not only balance the needs of the many stakeholders associated with their institution, both locally and nationally, but also to manage their relationships with key individuals in a positive and constructive way.

This assumes, of course, an ethic that places importance on the needs of all stakeholders and on constructive relationships. Without this moral dimension, an instinct for opportunity may manifest itself in rampant self-interest and corruption. Opportunism becomes the vehicle for advancing the career or financial interests of particular individuals, for example by choosing high-profile projects which do little for the long-term success of the college. If leaders are perceived as using their instinct for opportunity in order to turn people's worlds upside down in the interests of their own career and then move on, then economic arguments for change will rightly be treated with extreme cynicism (Lumby and Tomlinson, 2000).

Issues for the Lifelong Learning sector

Perhaps the most obvious, if slightly controversial, issue raised by this leadership theme is the sector's response to the Foster Report and the White Paper *Further Education: Raising skills, improving life chances* (DfES, 2006). To what extent will colleges and similar organisations regard this potentially radical agenda for change as the opportunity to pursue a strategy for change that meets the needs of multiple stakeholders, not just the government? Will some choose to resist the external pressure, waiting for political changes to shift the priorities or for lack of time and money to simply drain momentum from the whole initiative? Where is the real opportunity here? And which leaders will be most successful at spotting it and exploiting it?

Self-evaluation and development

So how's *your* instinct for opportunity? Here are some questions which will encourage you to reflect on this aspect of your leadership role and to evaluate your own strengths and areas for development.

● How much time do you spend each month, say, actively keeping up to date with political and economic changes affecting the sector?

● What is your involvement in the local community? How well can you claim to understand the local employment market and likely changes in the need for key skills?

● Are you someone who keeps in touch with a large and diverse group of acquaintances, or do you prefer to stick to a close-knit circle of like-minded people?

- How much time do you spend looking at other organisations, or other departments within your own organisation, in order to check on good practice?

- Do you enjoy experimenting with new approaches and stepping outside your 'comfort zone' occasionally, or would you rather stick with what you know works?

- How many times this week have you suggested how something might be improved?

- How would you rate your ability to read people's feelings or anticipate their likely response to a situation or proposal?

As ever, some of these things we may be able to change and some will be more 'hard-wired' into our psyche. If you are someone who struggles to see the bigger picture, you may be able to improve this by getting yourself involved in projects that require a more external, strategic perspective. On the other hand, you may decide that your keen eye for the detail is too important to dilute. In this case, call upon more naturally divergent-thinking colleagues to regularly challenge your perspective and ensure you recognise the value of those who may miss the detail but do come up with highly provocative insights and ideas.

Some of us are natural rationalists, who like to sift the data and be convinced by a reasoned argument before we go doing anything as rash as taking a risk. We regard our more instinctive colleagues as 'flying by the seat of their pants' and resent them for it, particularly when they succeed. But even we may be encouraged to stretch our 'comfort zone', perhaps with the help of a mentor, to take the odd calculated risk, and to think seriously about how we might work productively with those who may be more impulsive and creative than we are.

For many leaders, particularly lower down the hierarchy, the chance to take a wider perspective on the aims of the department or organisation may seem out of reach, and yet there are many straightforward ways we can improve our exposure to the environment in which our institution operates. So, what strategies can someone in a busy leadership role use in order to ensure they have an accurate and current overview of national and local developments? There are a number of ways to do this, and perhaps you implement all or most of them already. They include strategies such as:

- asking people who are likely to know – this will involve creating and sustaining your own networks within and outside the organisation;

- scanning the education press on a weekly basis – this can be less onerous than it sounds if you access the relevant websites and check the headline news for the sector;

- accessing other relevant websites regularly – these will include the DfES site, LSC, QIA, LLUK and the Association of Colleges (AoC);

- getting yourself registered on all the relevant e-mail lists accessible through these sites – this will provide you with breaking news and regular updates;

- attending conferences, launches and consultation events – this will not only keep you updated, but will also extend your network contacts.

And when you find yourself in possession of new or useful information, don't just hang on to it. Communicate it wherever appropriate. If you don't do that, you're not really being a networker, you're just being a sponge.

Summary of key points

In this chapter we have:

- considered the qualities and strategies which enable a leader to effectively identify and interpret 'environmental' issues which are key to their role and purpose;
- emphasised the importance of being a 'first-class noticer';
- suggested useful strategies for data and situation analysis;
- looked at ways of communicating the operational context to your team;
- suggested ways for you to evaluate your own skills and knowledge against Key Area A of the Occupational Standards.

4. Telling a compelling story

Introduction

Ask most people in leadership positions what their role is all about and the chances are that, early on, most of them will mention providing direction and aligning the team behind a common aim. Some, mainly those in more senior positions, may talk about vision or mission statements or strategy.

For effective leaders, a major part of their role is to bring everything together for people and help them to make sense of it (Jameson, 2006). They provide meaning and purpose. They make their teams feel part of something great and worthwhile. They help people to understand the challenges faced by the organisation and to see how they can contribute to addressing them. They may not be able to remove uncertainty and ambiguity, because that is part of what organisations must respond to, but they can help their teams to come to terms with it.

However, such talk also disguises a range of often contradictory approaches to the business of leadership. What is called vision or mission can be just as much an instrument of control, the blinkered complacency of an isolated leadership elite, the unoriginal and ultimately empty maxims of some well-meaning attempt to 'tick' the right leadership 'boxes'. Several managers in FE have remarked to us on the similarity between college mission statements.

Nevertheless, the best leaders have mastered the art of telling a compelling story. They provide direction where required, yes. But, more importantly, they create a working environment where values, purpose, policies and processes feel aligned and consistent, with the result that people can have the freedom to make decisions and take action for themselves. Furthermore, these leaders are adept at managing their *own* 'story'. They have a clear and accurate self-image and are not bashful about promoting this in ways that help to increase their influence and provide a positive role model to others.

So in this chapter we shall be addressing the following questions about how good leaders help us to make sense of the work we do as well as presenting a strong and consistent picture of themselves to which followers can relate.

- What is the difference between vision, values, purpose and mission, and what use are they?
- How can leaders use these to construct an enabling rather than a controlling environment?
- What does 'storytelling' mean at different levels of leadership?
- How much is it about selling and persuasion?
- What can happen if storytelling is used cynically and for the wrong reasons?
- How can we manage our own image and reputation as leaders in a positive and constructive way?

The case for meaning in leadership

Once upon a time, most successful organisations probably had a plan. At some point, this became too pedestrian and everyone, including the local butchers, was made to feel as though they also needed a strategy. Now, on top of a strategy, we all need a vision, a mission, values and goodness knows what else. Is this management-speak gone mad, or is any of it actually helpful?

Certainly there seems to be an overwhelming consensus among researchers and writers on leadership that effective leaders help people to understand what they and the organisation are about. Bennis and Nanus cite the *management of meaning* as one of their four leadership competencies, what Bennis elsewhere refers to as *creating a sense of mission* (Bennis, 2004; Bennis and Nanus, 1985). In their analysis of transformational leadership, one of Bass and Avolio's four Is is Inspirational motivation, which is all about providing meaning as well as challenge (Bass and Avolio, 1994). For some time, motivational theory has suggested that there is a higher order of need, known as self-actualisation, which stems in part from finding meaning in one's work, and, if met, should lead to high levels of satisfaction and productivity. Early attempts to 'tap into' this phenomenon involved job enrichment and job rotation, but the objective was the same: to make work more meaningful. Sadly, empirical evidence that any of it worked has generally been somewhat thin on the ground, although more recent research has suggested that 'voluntary employee effort' is encouraged by a sense of worth in one's job (Morris, 1996). It is still, however, something of a cross between common sense, anecdotal experience and employee feedback which leads us to believe that people make a more productive and creative contribution to organisations when they experience some sense of shared purpose.

The idea that we can overcome people's self-interest as a principal motivator by sharing some greater common purpose is definitely appealing (Barrett, 1998; Senge, 1990). However, an alternative view might be that shared vision and values actually serve our self-interest by making us feel good about what we do at work, especially if they are used to allow us more freedom in how we do our jobs. A well-defined purpose and mission, common values and shared goals can create an environment where people are more capable of managing themselves and performing well *together* (Drucker, 2001).

Some leadership thinkers identify a need for leaders to actively *sell the future*, using their persuasive arts to appeal to emotional as well as rational argument (Grint, 1999). This is echoed in some of the PCE-specific accounts as well, with principals talking of selling ideas (Lumby and Tomlinson, 2000).

Other commentators find the idea of selling a tad too close to manipulation, and prefer to talk of *enrolling* people in a vision, suggesting a little more informed choice on the part of followers (Senge, 1990).

Defining the way we tell stories

Given that terms like 'mission' and 'vision' are bandied around rather loosely, it might help to look more closely at what they mean.

- *Vision.* Senge refers to vision as the 'What?' because it describes the sort of future we wish to create. Richard Barrett sees the vision statement as a way of describing how the organisation achieves fulfilment. It is about the 'end', what you want to achieve (Senge, 1990; Barrett, 1998).

- *Mission.* This is sometimes used as another word for overall objective, what the organisation seeks to achieve, which explains why it readily gets muddled with vision. Others treat it as synonymous with purpose, in that it answers the question 'Why does this organisation exist?' The main intention of the mission here is to define the core business of the organisation.

- *Values.* If the vision is the 'What?' and the mission is the 'Why?', then values try to capture the 'How?' Values should articulate the beliefs and principles that guide how we act in achieving the vision – how we act towards each other, towards our students, towards partners, regulatory agencies and so on. They are one of the building blocks of the organisation's culture, and can vary from very pragmatic statements about what is important to the institution to an over-arching moral and ethical framework. Not surprisingly, therefore, they can be an important element in our 'moral compass'.

Of course, if all this still feels a bit like different ways of defining the same thing, you might prefer the approach taken by Collins and Porras in their book *Built to last*. They crystallise all of this into the concept of a *vision framework*, which consists of a core ideology describing the lasting characteristics of the organisation, *core values* and a *core purpose*, along with a description of the future and ambitious, long-term objectives which they refer to as *big, hairy, audacious goals* (Collins and Porras, 1994). The point that they make about this is that the core items are unlikely to change significantly whereas vision and goals may need to be more flexible and are subject to external pressures.

Whatever you choose to call them, however, it would seem that the story we tell as leaders is more engaging and motivating if it has three key elements:

● a description of what we are all aiming to achieve in the longer term;

● a sense of why we are here, what our organisation is for;

● some common view about what we think is important and the shared beliefs which guide how we act.

How we go about creating vision and purpose

So, how does this actually look 'on the ground'? We spoke to a number of leaders at various levels in FE colleges about vision and making meaning of what is going on and discovered some interesting differences of view. Our observations from all this would be as follows.

● Vision and storytelling can operate at all levels. We met programme leaders who had developed a vision for their specific team.

● While the senior management and principal may have a clear *vision framework*, this is not always understood by those lower down the organisation, and, if it is, it does not necessarily resonate with them.

● Vision and mission statements are often seen as rather anodyne and 'vanilla-flavoured', even by the senior management team.

● This is often because they are seen as determined by government policy rather than truly owned by the organisation.

● Broad, general statements of intent like this may be viewed lower down the organisation as more significant for what they *avoid* telling staff than for making their work meaningful.

● As a result of frustration with constructing meaningful vision statements, some senior managers opt for a different approach, focusing on core values and associated behaviours instead, or opting for broad themes that define what aspects of their institution are most important to them.

When it comes to *how* one engages staff in the creation of this 'story', there are clearly a number of problems. Perhaps because vision and mission are so wrapped up with direction and strategy, it is tempting to take a very 'top-down' approach to the process. The principal and the board lock themselves in a darkened room with copious amounts of coffee and biscuits and craft a statement that will not upset anyone. There then follows an attempt at 'involvement', which might vary from simply e-mailing the statement to all staff and effectively requesting their acquiescence to actually getting a few more managers round a table to discuss it. Either way, human nature suggests that, having sweated blood over constructing the vision in the first place, the board will be reluctant to make any great changes to it.

Research into vision in small and medium-sized enterprises by Warwick University's Manufacturing Group confirmed that the creation of a vision for the sake of it, without a need for change, resulted only in lip service. Collaboration outside the team of 'executive leaders' was essential for the success of the process (Craner, 2004). Visions that are inflexible and brook no alternative views are frequently those that die the swiftest. People fail to unite behind them, they remain unconvinced of their achievability and see current reality as conflicting entirely with the version of events being sold to them (Senge, 1990). The single-mindedness that many would see as a positive consequence of clear vision may thus become a drawback. In denying conflicting views and constructive debate, the organisation prevents people engaging with its aims and stunts its ability to adapt to its environment. The idea of leaders having a vision and then going off and aligning people with it becomes 'bankrupt', (Heifetz and Laurie, 2001).

The danger is that, without staff involvement, a leader may be seen as striding too far ahead of the team. And yet, ironically, this involvement can, at the same time, be hard to win, because the team themselves see vision as the leader's job. Achieving commitment rather than compliance depends on people being 'enrolled' in the vision, and in many organisations even the leaders do not feel this way, so it is hardly surprising that staff as a whole remain largely indifferent (Senge, 1990; Lumby and Tomlinson, 2000).

TASK

Let us at this point drop in on Lilly, Head of School of Communications, who is chairing one of her regular monthly section meetings with Graham's team:

Lilly   *OK, that brings us to item 4 on today's agenda, 'Mission and Values'. The Senior Management Team have been looking very hard at this, and we think we've got something now that the board will buy into. I'll just read it to you: 'Winterhill College believes in continuously striving for excellence in education, training and skills for business.'*

   Views?

Sunni   *What happened to widening community participation and all that?*

Lilly   *Well, Sunni, that's a couple of years old now. I mean it pre-dates the Foster Report, and, well, I think the team just thought we needed something a bit more focused.*

Graham	*To be honest, the widening participation thing must have completely passed me by. What was it before that then?*
Parminder	*Well I'm pleased to say that some of us take notice of these things, Graham. Before the widening participation thing it was something about a community of learning that values the individual.*
Graham	*Actually, I do remember that one. It was just before we shut three schools and made 300 people redundant.*
Lilly	*Oh, for goodness sake, can we move on? The point about mission is that it can change and adapt to circumstances.*
Sunni	*I thought the point about mission was that it didn't really change much.*
Lilly	*Did you really? Well tell that to the government. Can I take it that you're all happy with the mission? We've got three more agenda items to get through yet.*
Graham	*It sounds like craven political pandering to me. I resent not even being consulted.*
Lilly	*Thanks, Graham. I'll note it down as a three to one majority in favour.*
Sunni	*Never mind, Graham. You never take much notice of the mission statement anyway, and at least this one will see you into retirement.*
Graham	*I doubt it. I've still got six months to go!*
Lilly	*Settle down now, children. I'm just handing round the proposed college values. These are Suporting Students, Promoting Partnership, Delivering Diversity, Investing in Value and . . . well, something with buildings, but we couldn't think of anything beginning with B . . .*
Graham	*I might have a suggestion . . .*

What does this exchange tell you about the college's approach to telling a compelling story? Despite the history, what could Lilly have done differently to get people more on board with the idea? If you were on the SMT, what would you be advocating that the college do to enrol its staff in a common sense of purpose and a shared set of values? How would you address the inevitable scepticism that exists about such initiatives? Are the Grahams of this world right?

DISCUSSION

There is no easy answer to this dilemma. Maybe that is why some of the managers we spoke to preferred to focus on values and behaviours or themes because these felt more meaningful and lent themselves more easily to some process of dialogue with staff. They also avoid the impression that someone at the top knows all the right answers, and therefore they encourage more debate. Equally, the way we tell the story may denote different approaches to the job of leadership. Those who see it as primarily about setting direction and strategy may favour visions and mission statements, while those who interpret their role as being largely about building capability within the team may prefer to focus on values and behaviours. The attractiveness of the Collins and Porras *vision framework* (see page 48) is that it acknowledges the balance between consistency of values and purpose, and flexibility of vision and direction. However, there is no doubt that an overarching view of why the organisation exists and what sort of future it wants to create can be hugely motivating if it is genuinely shared by most employees (Kouzes and Posner, 1995). Ways of achieving this might include:

- initiating a 'bottom-up' process instead of, or in parallel with, senior management discussions, asking team leaders to discuss ideas with staff and obtaining feedback;
- adopting a more flexible approach to consulting on senior management views, perhaps drafting some unfinished ideas as bullet points and convening staff discussion groups before finalising any thoughts;
- presenting people with a number of options rather than the finished article, so that they have a sense of genuinely contributing to the debate;
- above all, accepting that this is a lengthy process that may take a long time and go through several iterations in order to achieve a meaningful dialogue. It is not a box to be ticked. It is hard work.

Telling a compelling story at every level

If you were thinking that all this vision and values stuff is the sole preserve of principals and chief executives and their immediate teams, then hopefully the preceding section will have convinced you of how much they need this process to be shared with every leader in the organisation. It is not practical for a leader, or a leadership team, of an organisation with several thousand employees to tap into individual beliefs and values and make the work of every employee feel more focused and meaningful. Inevitably, at the level of the whole organisation, vision, purpose and values will, at best, be couched in terms that are general enough for everyone to identify with. Yet, if we are unable to find some fit between our own values and vision of the organisation and those being touted by our leaders, we are unlikely to feel hugely energised by them (Senge, 1990).

Leaders at all levels, therefore, can play a key role in mediating between organisational strategy, vision and values and the reality of working in their particular part of the enterprise (Briggs, 2001). Leaders who can really engage their team in a continuing discussion about how the vision, purpose and values relate to the work they do can have a tremendous effect on people's motivation. Conversely, a perceived lack of fit between an individual's value system and that of the organisation can be a major source of stress and work–life imbalance. A crucial function of middle managers and front-line leaders is to talk with people about their role and their contribution to the organisation and how they might match this to what truly motivates them.

The key here is alignment. The fact that every team leader goes off and frames their own vision and values with their team could just as easily be caused by frustration or outright disagreement with the efforts of senior management. This will result in a mess of conflicting objectives and priorities around the organisation and general confusion over what the future holds and what the institution stands for. The National Occupational Standards for leadership and management in the post-compulsory sector highlight the need for middle managers to *ensure vision is aligned to the corporate vision.* West has some helpful guidelines for team vision, the first of which is *consistency with organisational objectives* (West, 1994). The full set of elements around which a team vision may be constructed is summarised in Figure 4.1.

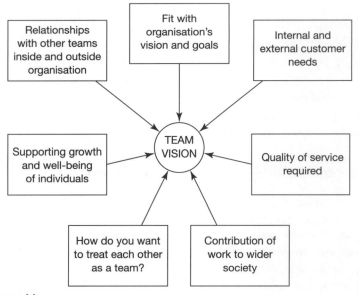

Figure 4.1 Team vision
(Adapted from West, 1994)

What is 'core' about you as a leader?

A leader's ability to tell a compelling story is not limited to the organisation, its aims and its values. They also have to be conscious of their own 'story'. We have already noted the importance of a good fit between personal and organisational values in the interests of both authenticity and sheer mental health. People are pretty good at spotting a phoney, and if you are to extol the vision of the future to which the organisation aspires and talk with your team about the values embodied in this vision, you had better be sure of where your belief system fits in with all this. How well do you model the sort of behaviours you are asking them to display?

Once again, self-awareness is key to effective leadership. This is not to say it has to be complete. Our journeys of self-discovery are generally work-in-progress and last most of our lives. But we have noted how good leaders not only have an accurate sense of who they are, and how they are perceived by others, but make skilful use of this in presenting themselves to the world.

Please do not misunderstand us. This is not about leaders making up impressive lies about themselves or becoming expert 'spin doctors' for their own reputation. Quite the contrary. A leader may conclude that being seen as quiet, thoughtful and low profile is not only fitting but also perfectly constructive. They will, however, exploit their individual style and 'voice' to make themselves more effective as a leader (Goffee and Jones, 2000). For example, one manager we interviewed unashamedly played on aspects of his previous background in order to establish credibility with employers and government. There may well be an element of performance about this, but no trace of dissembling, because it only works if it is authentic. Most effective leaders, while modestly suggesting you ask others about their strengths and weaknesses, will then proceed, in the next sentence, to give you a detailed rundown of what these are.

As a result, people often feel close to these leaders, because they feel that they know them, however remote they may be physically. They can relate to them, and that makes it much easier for the leader to make that connection with people that we talked about in Chapter 2.

CLOSE FOCUS

Think of a great leader, someone famous, or someone you have worked for. How well did you feel you knew them? What sort of things did they do that were 'typical' of them, and helped to define their individual leadership persona and 'voice'? Did this include acknowledging limitations?

This is not an argument for neglecting all attempts at self-improvement. As a leader, you may well have weaknesses you legitimately want to address. But none of us are perfect, and we all have 'allowable' weaknesses. Excellent leaders manage their reputation by incorporating all aspects of themselves and their experience, good and bad, into a consistent and grounded self-image. They know who they are, and they let you know who they are. They know what works for them, what is expected of them and what will influence their reputation (Goffee and Jones, 2000). As a result, they are generally at ease with themselves.

The 'dark side'

So, what happens when leaders tell great stories but lose their sense of moral and ethical direction? Strong vision and mission statements from on high can become a tool for imposing control and conformity rather than an invitation to take part in a noble venture. Used cynically, or just naively, they can have the effect of crushing opposition and imposing a dogma on the organisation that everyone is expected to obey regardless. *Nothing stifles openness more than certainty* (Senge, 1990).

In this world, single-mindedness becomes an unambiguous virtue and alternative views are not tolerated. Mission and vision become synonymous with a managerialist 'command and control' agenda.

Alternatively, the organisation becomes obsessed with 'spin' and public relations. When we talk about stories, we are using the term to denote a compelling piece of communication, but one that is decidedly non-fiction. For some, however, the scope for fiction, not to say outright fantasy here, is too much to resist. Leaders become 'snake-oil salesmen', flogging their remedies for the organisation's ills. They tell staff and the world outside what they think they want to hear while acting in direct conflict with their own words. Phoney leaders will exaggerate their abilities and disguise their shortcomings, talking their way into jobs and situations for which they are unprepared and unqualified. These are narcissistic leaders, puffed up with their own self-importance and an exaggerated view of their own abilities. If mistakes are made, the priority is how to allocate blame to someone else rather than how to solve the problem. This is a recipe for organisations and leaders that are all gloss and no substance.

Issues for the Lifelong Learning sector

The ability of leaders to construct a compelling story is an especially pointed issue in a sector which, by popular consensus, is still working to identify its true role. In the aftermath of the Foster Report and subsequent White Paper, institutions will need to decide if their response is limited to a superficial rewording of the vision and mission to fit in with latest 'strategy initiative' from central government, or a genuine attempt to engage staff in creating a shared view, a view of how the sector can play the most effective role and what this means for individual institutions and the values and behaviours to which they subscribe.

This also raises the issue of who is really in control of the 'story'. Leaders in Lifelong Learning may sometimes feel that the story is being woven not by them but by government (who themselves may or may not have a clear idea of how the story ends!), and that they can play only a limited role in mediating between national policy decisions and their teams. However, we would argue that this is to drastically underestimate the influence they can have, if not in shaping policy in every case, then at least in helping their team/department/ organisation make sense of what is going on.

Self-evaluation and development

What, then, can you do to navigate your own way through this particular aspect of leadership? Well, it would seem to make sense to start, as ever, with your own story.

So, ask yourself what is it about your background, experience and personality that makes you who you are? How does this help you do the job you do? What are your strengths and what are you not so good at? How can other people help?

Is the persona you inhabit at work very different from the one you inhabit at home with family and friends? If so, why do you think this is? Which one is the 'real' you? Are you comfortable with this? How might you be more like your real self at work? How would people respond if you took this risk?

One way to address this is to conduct a personal values inventory. What are the things you hold most dear in life? What does success mean to you? What makes you happy/angry? Do not just stop at answering these questions. Try using the 'four whys' technique, asking your self 'why?' as you answer each successive question, in order to drill down to the real core beliefs behind your attitudes to life and work (Barrett, 1998). Where is there a good fit between these values and the work you do? Where do they clash?

Finally, how does all this affect the way you behave as a leader? How can you build on and exploit the positive aspects of this? What do you want to be really known for? What is the unique combination of expertise, personality, experiences and allowable weaknesses that enables you to do your job well? Which situations will play most strongly to this self-image, and what more can you do to leverage the usefulness of this in helping you become more effective in your job? You might find that a skilful coach or mentor can help you undertake this process by structuring the discussion and providing some challenge and objectivity.

Having looked at *yourself* more closely, how do you build a vision and purpose for the organisation? We do not propose to duplicate the wealth of excellent material on stakeholder analysis, SWOT (strengths, weaknesses, opportunites, threats) and all of the other specific techniques you might choose to employ when trying to decide what your institution is here for and what kind of future it hopes to create for itself. The strategy and organisational development books are full of great advice. From a personal leadership development angle, all we would say is, find a way of talking about this to a lot of people throughout the organisation. This will make it real and meaningful for them, but, equally importantly, will challenge you to ensure that this story is more than superficial. It will be polished and refined by rubbing up against other versions of reality within the organisation and people's personal values, including your own. It will help you to see the link between the vision and values you espouse and the way your behaviour is perceived by others.

Hopefully, this process, by telling you more about the kind of leader you are, will also reveal what kind of storytelling suits you best. Are you a natural orator who can address a large audience at the drop of a hat? Or do you need plenty of preparation before any public speaking and prefer smaller groups? If formal presentations are not your strong point, is this just a question of technique and training, or would you feel more comfortable making a virtue of this by adopting a deliberately informal style? If you are just not good at talking to groups, are you happier with more of a question and answer approach to addressing teams? How do you feel about admitting to your dislike of speech-making and focusing instead on becoming highly effective in small-group or one-to-one meetings?

Summary of key points

- Excellent leaders help to weave a motivating story around what the organisation is trying to achieve and what it believes in.
- They also know enough about their own values, strengths and limitations to present a consistent and accurate self-image to the outside world. People know what they stand for.
- They nurture this authentic and individual leadership 'voice', exploiting it in ways that enhance their effectiveness in the role.
- They help people to make sense of their own contribution to the organisation and its goals by engaging in a continuing dialogue. They create a sense of truly shared vision and values.
- They use the 'story' to provide individuals and teams with a consistent framework within which to take decisions and respond to change on their own initiative.

5. Developing self and teams 1: reflective leadership

CHAPTER OBJECTIVES

This chapter is designed to help you to:

- take a reflective approach to self-development;
- examine the importance of prioritising and realistic action planning;
- consider ways in which you can assess your own performance and identify your own development needs;
- consider the importance of seeking and responding to feedback;
- analyse ways in which the characteristics of your team, the requirements of your job and the mission of the organisation will shape your own development needs;
- evaluate your own skills and knowledge against Key Area C of the Occupational Standards;
- create a climate of learning and improvement for your team.

Introduction

This chapter is about reflective leadership. It is about the ways in which you can develop yourself and your own professional performance. Elsewhere in this book we have written at length about the adaptive capacity of great leaders, their inclination to take calculated risks when required, to question the status quo and challenge themselves and those around them. We've stressed the importance of self-knowledge and of retaining an awareness of our own strengths and weaknesses. The leaders we spoke to in FE were aware of their strengths, but also aspects of their approach that their team might find frustrating. In other words, they had thought about their experiences and tried to form an accurate picture of themselves. They seemed to accept that, given the uncertain nature of what lay ahead for the Lifelong Learning sector, their most effective strategy was flexibility and a readiness to continue to learn and adapt. This is why in virtually every chapter we have devoted a section to your self-development, asking questions to help you to determine your own performance in relation to the particular leadership themes we have described, and hopefully offering some guidance as to how you might further develop your own unique approach to this aspect of the leadership role. Much of this has focused on the sort of person you are, and how you might adapt your leadership to your own natural strengths. However, as we argued at the start, leaders are both born and made. Much of this chapter, therefore, is designed to help you reflect on what you do and how you might continue to improve it.

Reflective practice

As a way of assessing your own performance, reflective practice is an essential tool for everyone with leadership responsibilities in FE. What do we mean by 'reflective practice', exactly? Reflective practice, like emotional intelligence, is a way of working rather than an end in itself. When, after a long day's work, we find ourselves going over in our minds some incident or encounter which stands out for us, there are three ways we can choose to respond to it. We can go over it again and again in a descriptive way like an endless series of TV repeats; we can push it out of our mind by going to the gym or watching some real television; or – and this is where reflective practice comes in – we can turn it into a positive learning experience by asking ourselves some hard questions about it. In other words, we don't just ask ourselves *What happened*? but also the following questions:

- Is there anything about that incident/encounter/meeting/set of figures/etc. I would like to change?
- If so, why?
- What could I realistically have done to change it?
- If there's nothing I'd want to change, why did it work so well?
- Is there a general principle here that I can put into practice again next time I'm faced with a similar incident/task?

Many professionals find it useful to keep a reflective journal, as part of their formal professional development plan, in which they can jot down and track this sort of reflection. This comes in useful when you move to the next stage, where you put some of your reflections to the test. For example, imagine you have chaired a disastrous meeting in which voices became raised, the agenda ignored and the timing drastically overrun (we've probably all experienced one of those). Do you fume all evening, blaming the fiasco on the inappropriate behaviour of unruly colleagues? No. After some reflection – after asking yourself all the key questions listed above – you come to the conclusion that, as chair, you should have laid down much tighter parameters at the beginning of the meeting and reminded everyone present that they must address all remarks through the chair. Next time you find yourself leading a meeting, you put this hypothesis to the test, and afterwards you reflect again. How well did it work? Why? How could you revise or refine your modus operandi next time? And so on. The next stage is the crucial one, because – remember – we're not talking simply about reflection here but about reflective practice. You can have as many insights and bright ideas as you like, but if, like an armchair general, you never actually put them to the test, they will be of limited value to your professional development.

This model of reflective practice is, essentially, the same as the one we would use to describe what happens in education action research. It can be expressed most simply as in Figure 5.1.

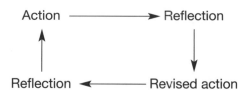

Figure 5.1 *Model of reflective practice*

TASK

Let's have a look now at a couple of examples of colleagues, thinking about critical incidents in their working day. What we'd like you to do is to identify whether they are being analytical and reflective, or simply descriptive. You may find it useful to jot down the evidence to support your answers so that you can compare them with ours in the discussion which follows. First, here's an extract from the reflective journal that Costas is keeping as part of his MA in Educational Leadership and Management.

> *Our LSC [Learning and Skills Council] is about to publish its new Strategic Plan for post-compulsory education and training in the local area. I overheard two of my team talking this morning about a rumour that part of the plan will be to concentrate funding for skills training on the bigger FE colleges on the other side of the county and cut funding to our college so that we're forced into a merger with one of the others. This is rubbish, of course. I'm staff rep on the Board of Corporation and we've seen drafts of the Plan in progress. There's nothing sinister going on. But people don't seem to listen to sense once rumour's got a hold. I interrupted these two and told them they were worrying about nothing. The trouble is, once a rumour like this gets going, it affects everybody's morale, and eventually it's going to leak into the wider community, and that's where it starts doing the real damage – undermining confidence in the college. Perhaps I should have called a meeting to contradict the rumour and reassure people. Put an e-mail round, maybe? Too late now though, probably.*

DISCUSSION

So, is Costas reflecting, or simply describing what's going on? The answer is that there's very little practice-related reflection here. He begins by setting out a factual account of what's happened and what he knows about it. Then he goes on to comment on the destructive effects of rumour. Finally he reflects on what he might have done differently:

> Perhaps I should have called a meeting to contradict the rumour and reassure people. Put an e-mail round, maybe?

But he doesn't link this to any future action. He ends with a verbal shrug about it probably being 'too late' to do anything about it. In terms of reflective practice – that is *planned practice arising from reflection* – there's nothing here. All we've got is a bit of reflection arising from practice, with no link to future action or development.

There are several issues he could have reflected on in order to plan possible strategies for the future. He could have considered what might be the most effective means of spotting a rumour, challenging a rumour, sustaining the morale of staff, sustaining the credibility of the organisation, implementing damage limitation and so on, and he could have planned out how and when he would try these strategies in practice. By failing to do so, he loses the opportunity to turn a critical incident into an opportunity for personal professional development.

CLOSE FOCUS

Rumour can have a very destructive effect in an organisation such as an FE college, particularly when staff are feeling the stress of working in a climate of constant change. Take some time to reflect on how you would respond if you discovered such a rumour doing the rounds in your own section, school or faculty. What skills, strategies or qualities would you need to bring into play? Can you identify any action points for your own professional development plan that arise from these reflections?

TASK

Now read through this entry in Jean's journal. She's had a chance to read this chapter and, as Head of Faculty, is interested in encouraging reflective practice. But is she practising it herself? Can you identify any examples which are reflective rather than simply descriptive? Again, you may like to jot down some notes and then compare your answer to what we have to say in the discussion below.

Two of my Heads of School are at loggerheads. When they're not arguing at Faculty Management Group (FMG) meetings, they're sitting glaring at each other. It seems that whatever line Orson takes, Lilly will take the opposite. This all makes everyone uncomfortable. The trouble is, I do find it difficult to remain impartial. Orson and his wife are personal friends of mine, and Orson is always a very supportive colleague. He is also popular with his subject team, and their retention and achievement figures are always excellent. Lilly, on the other hand, has an abrasive manner and she's made some decisions recently which I think raise questions about her judgement. And, what's more, her team always seem generally miserable and demotivated. We've got an OFSTED inspection coming up, so really this is crunch time. I've got to find some way to resolve all this. I think the answer must start with a serious conversation with Orson and with Lilly (separately). This is going to be really difficult, and if I'm honest I'd have to say that's why I've been shelving this problem and just hoping it'll go away. I'm not good at confrontation, and it's difficult to see how I'm going to avoid it in this situation. I'm going to need every ounce of people skills I possess. And I think the danger may be that I'll either be too conciliatory (just to avoid confrontation), or too confrontational (just to avoid being too conciliatory!). So I need to be clear about what I say to each of them. And I need to keep the meeting with Orson on a professional footing and not let our personal relationship seep into it. I think I'll start by asking him to think about the implications and collateral damage arising from this running battle with Lilly, for the teams, the Faculty, for me and for him. And I think I'll ask him to go away and think about it and then fix a time to meet later the same day to sit down and discuss what we can do about it. That way I won't be appearing to ambush him or put him on the spot. And actually, I think I'll do the same with Lilly. I think it's probably quite important that I treat them exactly the same, so that Lilly can't accuse me of favouritism. And then, hopefully, we can have a further meeting, with all three of us there, to discuss how we're going to work as a united team to prepare for the inspection. Yes, that's the strategy I'm going to try. And I'm not going to put it off. I'm going to do it tomorrow.

DISCUSSION

This journal entry demonstrates that Jean does indeed have a clear understanding of reflective practice. Here we have a classic pattern.

- What's happened or is happening?
- What are the issues?
- What do I need to do about it? (*I think the answer must start with a serious conversation with Orson and with Lilly*)
- How does it relate to my professional development? (*I'm not good at confrontation*)
- How does this translate into a plan for action? (*I think I'll start by asking him to think about the implications and collateral damage of this running battle with Lilly . . . etc.*)

In other words, Jean is not only being reflective, but also *her planning of her future practice is based on that reflection.* She is demonstrating, in this situation at least, the art of reflective leadership.

CLOSE FOCUS

Do you agree with Jean's planned approach? Certainly it's not the only option open to her. What strategies would you advise her to take, and why?

We shall revisit this situation with Jean's Faculty Management Group in Chapter 7 and look at its implications from a slightly different perspective.

Seeking and responding to feedback

Reflective practice is an essential tool for leadership in FE. Often, however, reflecting alone is not enough to enable you to accurately identify your own areas for professional development. Seeking and reflecting on the feedback of others is a useful way to ensure that your evaluation of your own strengths and weaknesses is realistic and sufficiently objective. Furthermore, as a leader, seeking feedback is a very public way of setting an example. It demonstrates to your team that everyone can continue to learn and improve, and, done properly, it helps to create a climate where performance can be discussed without fear. By acknowledging that you may make mistakes and need to learn from them, you give others permission to risk failure in the interests of getting better at what they do.

If you have a mentor, they are the ideal person to provide you with such feedback and to help you to think through your action plan for professional development. If you don't have a mentor, you may like to request one, either as a formal part of your continuing professional development or as an informal arrangement with a trusted colleague whose views and judgement you know you can trust. Such a colleague will be acting as a 'mentor' even though you may not refer to them by that label. We have much more to say about the role of the mentor – official and unofficial – in the next chapter because it's a role that you yourself are likely to play, formally or informally, as the leader of your team.

Asking for feedback about our professional performance can feel like a very high-risk strategy. What if we hear something negative about an aspect of our work that we assumed was well up to standard? What if we hear a criticism with which we're unable to agree? How do we avoid taking this personally or sinking into despondency? Let's see how Gordon handles this.

Jean	*So how do you think that went, Gordon? Are you happy with the way you handled that meeting?*
Gordon	*Yeah. I thought it went quite well, actually. Rob talked too much, as usual, but . . .*
Jean	*He did, didn't he? Do you think there was anything you could have done about that?*
Gordon	*Well, once he gets going . . .*
Jean	*Yes, but he went on far too long and people were getting fed up. And in the end there wasn't enough time to discuss some of the important agenda items. You were the chair, so what could you have done about that?*
Gordon	*Shot him?*
Jean	*No, seriously. What could you have done?*
Gordon	*I don't know. If I could think of something, I'd have done it, wouldn't I?*
Jean	*Come on. Don't get cross. I thought you wanted some feedback.*
Gordon	*OK. Sorry. You're right. Well, I suppose I could have butted in, thanked him, and invited someone else to comment.*

Jean	*Exactly. As chair it's part of your responsibility to see that everybody gets a chance to air their view. If this means chopping somebody off when they've gone on too long, so be it.*
Gordon	*That's what you do. I like the way you chair meetings. They never go on too long.*
Jean	*Thank you!*
Gordon	*So I suppose that's why I chose you to give me some feedback. Thanks for that, Jean.*
Jean	*You're very welcome.*

Gordon handled that quite well in the end, didn't he? He realised that it's no good asking for feedback and expecting to receive only praise. The areas for development are what we need to hear about, because it's only by recognising and addressing those that we can move forward in our professional development. It also helps set the tone for how 'cries for help' are regarded within the team. For many of the leaders we interviewed, the crime was not finding a task difficult, but finding it difficult and keeping quiet about it. They welcomed requests for help as an opportunity to help people develop. But they could only do this by demonstrating through their own example that it is OK to ask for help in the first place. Effective leaders, as we stressed in Chapter 2, are not afraid of showing their weaknesses, nor of asking for advice and assistance when necessary. That's why we talk about seeking and *responding* to feedback, and why the Occupational Standards stress the need to *obtain* and act upon *feedback from appropriate people to further improve performance* (LLUK, 2005, our emphasis).

It's also significant that Gordon 'chose' Jean as the person he wanted to give him feedback. You'll see from the organisation chart in the Appendix that Jean isn't his line manager, isn't even in the same faculty. He's chosen her to evaluate his ability to chair a meeting because he admires the way she herself chairs them. In this way he is taking responsibility for his own professional development by seeking out the best role model from whom to receive some unofficial mentoring.

Prioritising and action planning

The direction your own professional development needs to take will also be dependent, to some extent, on the strengths – and otherwise – of your team as a whole, and on the purpose and direction of the organisation within which you work. For example, if the team you currently lead is very strong on marketing expertise but you yourself are not, it might be more useful for you to focus your efforts on some other underdeveloped aspect of your professional skills and knowledge – financial management, for example – which is lacking right across your team. Similarly, taking the purpose of the organisation into account, there would be little point in prioritising the further development of your skills in Adult Education if the college's plan is to focus the efforts of your school or department on provision for 14–16 year olds.

Your action plan for your own professional development, therefore, will be based largely upon:

- your own evaluation of your performance;
- feedback from appropriate sources;
- the human resource requirements within your team;
- the direction and purpose of the college as a whole.

Managing your time effectively

Of course, in order to effectively put your action plan for your own professional development into practice you will first have to be able to ring-fence some *time* in which to make it happen. Sometimes it will seem to you – as it does to most people with leadership roles in FE – as though all your time is already spoken for. This can be a very stressful way to perceive things. Some have described it as like being in the backseat of a speeding car, knowing where you want to go, but having absolutely no control over the brakes or steering. In fact, time management may seem like one of your most difficult challenges. This is probably because 'managing time' really is an impossibility. It's *yourself* you need to manage and the *way that you use your time*. Take a look at Chapter 7 for a few ideas on ways of getting yourself more organised.

The 'dark side'

There are a number of ways in which a faulty 'moral compass' may manifest itself with regard to a leader's approach to learning and improvement. Leaders may be brutally honest about their shortcomings and where they need help but strangely disinclined to do anything about it. As a result, they 'dump' on their team and constantly let them down. They make a virtue out of their 'hopeless' lack of aptitude in a particular area (or several), but neither address it nor find strategies to get round it. They just let others pick up the pieces.

At the other end of the scale is the leader who aspires to infallibility, finding excuses or others to blame rather than being honest about mistakes. This encourages a fear of admitting errors throughout the team or organisation. High standards translate themselves into an intolerance of failure rather than an invitation to keep getting better. Without an open acceptance of failure, improvement is stifled and the organisation ceases to learn. Or perhaps the leader is just afraid to admit to any weaknesses because they feel this will undermine their authority. Consequently, their team comes to regard them as 'unassailable' and is nervous about asking for help or suggesting new ideas.

Issues for the Lifelong Learning sector

Although this chapter addresses individual development, there are implications for performance improvement at individual, team and organisational level. The debate around standards and measurement throughout the education sector, and the increasing emphasis on performativity and outputs within Lifelong Learning in particular, have raised important questions as to what really works. From formal appraisal to national standards, is an emphasis on measurement obscuring the need for continuous reflection and improvement? Or, without such solid evaluation processes, are we in danger of falling further behind in the international competitiveness league? Are we measuring the right things, and does the current approach encourage openness or inhibit it? How can leaders in Lifelong Learning help create 'learning organisations' where questioning and experimentation and continuous improvement are seen as more important than avoiding 'cock-ups' and doing as you are told?

Self-evaluation and development

So, how do you rate yourself as a reflective leader? When was the last time you asked for feedback from:

- peers?
- your boss?
- your team?
- a mentor/coach?

If so, how did it feel? Were you able to be positive about it?

How do you feel about asking team members for help, or revealing when there is something you do not feel entirely confident of dealing with? Do you treat your mistakes and those of others as an opportunity to learn or as a frustrating setback in an already crowded day? How does your team feel about asking you for help or admitting when they cannot cope? Have you asked them?

In common with many leaders, you may find it difficult to reconcile setting high standards for yourself and your team with the idea of getting things wrong or asking for help. How might you reframe things in your own mind to help with this? Perhaps demonstrating continuous improvement in your own performance can be seen as every bit as stretching an aim as never making a mistake? It is certainly a more realistic one.

Hopefully, throughout this chapter, we have given you some helpful ideas on how you might evaluate your own development needs and address them. If we had to get our advice on professional development into one soundbite it would probably be this:

> *The key to success lies in reflective practice, action planning and getting yourself a good mentor.*

Summary of key points

In this chapter we have:

- encouraged you to take a reflective approach to self-development;
- examined the importance of prioritising and realistic action planning;
- suggested ways in which you can assess your own performance and identify your own development needs;
- suggested some strategies which will help you to manage your own time more effectively;
- encouraged you to seek and respond to feedback;
- suggested ways in which the characteristics of your team, the requirements of your job and the mission of the organisation may shape your own development needs;
- discussed the importance of creating a climate of learning and improvement for your team;
- encouraged you to evaluate your own skills and knowledge against Key Area C of the Occupational Standards.

6. Developing self and teams 2: creating capability

Introduction

In the previous chapter we looked at issues related to your own professional development as a leader. In this chapter we explore ways in which you can foster the professional development of those individuals who make up your team and of the team as a whole. As a leader in the Lifelong Learning sector, this role as facilitator of others' learning and development will be one with which you are both familiar and comfortable. But this doesn't mean that it'll happen automatically without you having to think about it. The development of your team – like your own professional development – requires accurate analysis, timely action and careful monitoring. It's back to the familiar cycle of reflective development through action shown in Figure 6.1.

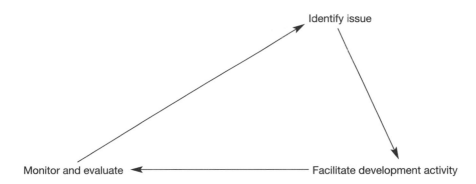

Figure 6.1 Reflective development through action

It will also require you to be familiar with two sets of standards: the SVUK (Standards Verification UK) Standards for Teaching and Supporting Learning, and the LLUK (Lifelong Learning UK) Occupational Standards for Leadership and Management.

Modelling good practice

We began this book with the question about whether good leaders are born or made and we've suggested that the answer is probably: it's a bit of both. But what about other aspects of the FE professional's role? Are good teachers born or made? Are efficient administrators/workplace liaison staff/mentors/assessors born that way, or do they need to be supported and developed? Well, it would be great if every member of your team was born to the job and all you had to do was organise the Christmas party. But that's not likely to be the case. Everyone is entitled to access professional development – however excellent their current performance – and some will need more development and support than others. Clearly, the best place to start is by looking at your own behaviour – as we encouraged you to do in the previous chapter – and making sure that you yourself are providing a model of good practice. Put at its simplest, this is a matter of being able to say, 'do what I do' rather than simply 'do what I say'. And, as we've agreed, good practice is about professionalism and values every bit as much as it's about performing competently to a national standard. This means that leading by example is about more than just getting the job done.

Let's have a look at Douglas, a head of section, giving a lead to Maya who is fairly new to teaching on his team and is in the process of gaining her Certificate in Education (PCET) through part-time in-house study.

Doug *Okay, Maya? How's it going?*

Maya *Hi. Not too bad. Teaching's fine. Can't get the hang of this 'Reflective Journal' thing we're supposed to do, though. What's all that about?*

Doug *Oh, I shouldn't worry about that. As long as the teaching's OK . . .*

Maya *And I'm having a bit of a problem with my planning. I can't get my head around this thing about differentiation. I don't suppose I could have a look at one of your lesson plans, could I, Doug? To see how to include differentiated activities?*

Doug *Erm . . .*

Maya *Because we've got to demonstrate how we differentiate in terms of learning activities and assessment. If I could just have a look at one of yours?*

Doug *Right. Well, as it happens, I don't bother much with differ . . . different . . .*

Maya *Differentiation.*

Doug *Right. I don't bother about it much myself.*

Maya *Really? Oh. Right. But it'd still be really useful if I could have look at how you set out your lesson plans.*

Doug	*Yeah. Well. Thing is, you know, no one really bothers with those once they've got the qualification.*
Maya	*So you don't have any plans for your lessons that you can show me?*
Doug	*Nah. You just don't bother with those after a while.*

Oh dear. We've probably all met 'Doug' in one guise or another. In this case it's not so much *What do you call a man with spade in his head?* as *What do you call a Section Leader with his foot in his mouth?* However effectively he functions in other aspects of his leadership role – for example, cheering people on, or getting the paperwork done – Doug's going to have real difficulties in facilitating the professional development of his team as long as he's failing to keep up to speed himself. And how can he expect Maya and others to commit themselves to the demanding and time-consuming process of professional development when his own behaviour and attitude are implicitly undermining the standards on which such development is based?

In leading by example, therefore, we need a convenient, shorthand way to think about the sort of model we're providing for those three key facets of professional practice in FE which apply to all roles at all levels within the organisation. It's useful to think of this as PAT:

- P for performance (meeting the required standard);
- A for attitude (enthusiasm, loyalty, reflective practice);
- T for team spirit (sharing organisational values, vision and goals).

Doug, as we've just seen, falls short in all three facets. He's not meeting the SVUK standards in planning and differentiation; he denies the importance of reflective practice; and in neglecting those two facets of his professional performance he is failing to contribute towards what must be the college's shared goal of excellence and meeting national standards.

This scenario illustrates clearly for us how easy it would be to provide the wrong kind of role model at the 'sharp' end of the organisation. But what about those in more senior leadership positions? Let's go right to the top now and see what Walter is up to.

Walter, the Principal of Winterhill College, is nearing retirement. He is a principal of the old school, having had no formal management training but having risen to his current post through internal promotion. He joined Winterhill College as a Senior Lecturer and Section Head 35 years ago, and has only ever worked in one other college, where he began his career in teaching. He has built up his leadership and management skills on the job and is a firm believer that that's the best way to do it. The requirement for all newly appointed principals to undertake, or have already undertaken, training in leadership and management (DfES, 2006) has been greeted by Walter with a great deal of cynicism, and he has been unsupportive – publicly as well as privately – of aspiring senior leaders within the college who have expressed a desire to undertake this sort of professional development.

It's quite easy to see here that Walter, surprisingly, has a great deal in common with Douglas. Neither of them is demonstrating full support for the current standards for the sector and thereby both of them are jeopardising the professional prospects of their teams. In terms of PAT (performance, attitude, team spirit), Walter may well be scoring P for performance in other aspects of his role as principal, but he's clearly failing in his loyalty to colleagues because he's obstructing their professional development in leadership, and he's ignoring the goals and vision of the sector because he's neglecting to foster the growth of new leaders. A very real issue for senior leadership currently is the issue of succession. And just in case you're about to ask us why we'd suddenly be talking about Prince Charles at this juncture, let's quickly point out to those of you who need reminding that the succession issue here is about the effective replacement of those many FE principals currently approaching retirement. Where will the new generation of expertise come from? How will potential successors gain the skills necessary for senior leadership in the Lifelong Learning sector of the twenty-first century? One of the ways, clearly, is for the current senior leadership to build capacity by encouraging aspiring principals to undertake appropriate professional development.

At all levels of the institution it is important to remember that 'creating capability' isn't just about ensuring that human resources are adequate to meet current needs. It's also about having an eye to the future and taking steps to ensure that there is a pool of suitably qualified, high-performing professionals whose career trajectory will allow them to step into the roles vacated by valued veterans who are retiring or moving on to new roles elsewhere.

Supporting the professional development of individuals

When it comes to supporting the development of each individual in your team, you will find there are a number of essential steps you will need to take with them. We can summarise them here as follows.

1. Provide an induction.
2. Monitor their performance.
3. Establish and maintain effective communication.
4. Agree achievable, measurable, specific objectives.
5. Negotiate support for achieving these objectives.
6. Review performance/outcomes against the agreed objectives and give constructive feedback.

One thing which may immediately strike you about this list is that points 3–6 are also a pretty good description of the process we usually call 'mentoring'. And this is no accident. As team leader you will inevitably find yourself in a mentoring role in relation to individuals within your team, and the skills and qualities necessary in a good leader overlap extensively with those necessary for effective mentoring, particularly in the area of communication.

Mentoring and coaching

Mentoring is currently receiving a lot of attention in the Lifelong Learning sector, not only because of the widespread use of mentoring for subject specialist support on teacher training programmes, but also because of the emphasis on continuing professional development for professionals at all levels of the FE organisation, as evidenced by the White Paper *Further Education: Raising skills, improving life chances* (DfES, 2006). This is an aspect of professional practice with which all leaders will need to familiarise themselves. For now, let's content ourselves with a couple of definitions and some pointers for good practice.

In the world outside FE the term *coaching* is often used to refer to the process of observation followed by discussion which is designed to improve performance (think of a sports coach), and *mentoring* as a series of dialogues in which the mentor helps the mentee to gain sufficient insight to evaluate their own performance. In FE, though, we tend to refer to both kinds of one-to-one support as *mentoring*. Of course, what we call it is far less important than that we do it effectively. For effective mentoring it is useful to follow some cardinal rules.

The relationship needs to be based on:

- trust;
- rapport;
- a shared agenda;
- the willingness to allow the mentee to make their own discoveries.

The mentoring sessions need to:

- be structured;
- adhere to mutually agreed ground rules;
- identify areas of opportunity as well as for development;
- involve and encourage experimentation and reflection;
- provide both support and challenge;
- lead to agreed action.

Above all, being a mentor is about getting people to *think*, not about providing them with the answers – not to the higher-order questions, anyway. Of course, if they're asking questions like, 'Where's the nearest photocopier?' you're going to have to tell them.

So let's go back to Maya, who's recognised the limited usefulness of turning to Doug for support and has instead approached Gordon, the Head of School, who has recently read a helpful book on mentoring in FE (Wallace and Gravells, 2005).

TASK

As you read through the dialogue below, see if you can identify where and how this mentoring session follows the cardinal rules we've just looked at.

Maya   *Oh hi, Gordon. Could you spare me a few minutes?*

Gordon   *Maya! Nice to see you. I've got exactly 15 minutes before my next meeting. Will that do?*

Maya   *Thanks. Yes. Thing is, Gordon, I'm having trouble with differentiation.*

Gordon   *Well, why don't you tell me about it.*

Maya   *I'm not exactly sure what it is, or how I'm supposed to get it into my lesson plans. Have you got a lesson plan of yours you can show me?*

Gordon   *Yes, but just tell me first what you understand differentiation to mean.*

Maya   *Having different activities and different outcomes for different learners in the same group?*

Gordon   *And why would we want to do that?*

Maya   *Erm, to cater for different learning needs?*

Gordon   *Such as?*

Maya   *Such as when some of the learners have already got quite good numeracy skills, but others haven't or aren't confident? So you don't want the good ones to get bored and you don't want the unconfident ones to get scared, so you prepare differentiated activities until they're all at least at the required standard?*

Gordon   *Absolutely. So you wanted to ask me about it, why?*

Maya   *I just wasn't sure. I feel much better now.*

Gordon   *Shall we fix another meeting for this time next week and in the meantime you can have a go at getting all that down in a lesson plan and then trying it out and having a think about how it went so you can talk me through it?*

Maya   *That'd be cool, Gordon. Thanks.*

DISCUSSION

You probably found that Gordon, as mentor, managed to tick nearly all the boxes.

- *Trust.* We can perhaps assume this, as Maya actively sought Gordon out.

- *Rapport.* The dialogue demonstrates courtesy and warmth on both sides. Again, as Maya sought Gordon out we may suppose she expected to feel some rapport with him.

- *A shared agenda.* Maya sets the agenda, which is one that Gordon, as her Head of School, surely shares as it impacts upon standards of teaching and supporting learning.

- *The willingness to allow the mentee to discover things for herself.* What Gordon does here is known as *Socratic questioning.* He asks Maya questions in order to help her realise that she herself already knows the answers to these questions. She is discovering her *tacit knowledge* and understanding of the issue that's been troubling her. This is far more empowering for Maya than if Gordon simply handed her all the answers.

- *Structure.* Gordon is quite clear about the parameters. He has 15 minutes to give her, and he flags this up at the outset. He also makes firm and clear arrangements for their next meeting.

- *Mutually agreed ground rules.* They didn't get on to this. Not surprising, given that they only had 15 minutes for this initial meeting. But the ground rules could have included, for example, Gordon not fishing to try to find out why Maya has come to him, not to Doug (they both seem to be imposing this ground rule on themselves independently, however, which is perhaps a measure of their professionalism), or not discussing issues of a personal nature.

- *Identifying areas of opportunity.* Gordon ensures the emphasis is upon the opportunities here for mentoring and development rather than upon Maya's lack of confidence about differentiation.

- *Encouraging experimentation and reflection.* Gordon encourages Maya to have a go, to try out some differentiation and then reflect on how well it worked, ready for their discussion next time.

- *Provide both support and challenge.* While friendly and helpful, Gordon presses Maya to think for herself (*tell me first what you understand it to mean*).

- *Agreed action.* In agreeing an objective or outcome – in the form of the lesson plan with differentiated activities – Gordon has ensured that their mentoring session was not simply all talk but resulted in clear goal-setting.

We can represent this process by means of the model shown in Figure 6.2.

Figure 6.2 Mentoring model
Source: (Wallace and Gravells, 2005)

Essential steps in providing professional development for individuals

Let's go back now to those steps we identified as essential to supporting individual professional development. As you read through them you will notice the close fit between these and the factors which are important for effective mentoring

1. Provide an induction

Do you remember your first days in your current organisation? You were probably provided with a comprehensive induction which included a detailed introduction to the policies, geography, working practices and key personnel of the college as a whole and your corner of it in particular. Possibly you were also provided with a staff handbook – or given access to one online – which encapsulated all the essential information you would need about your new place of work. If you were not so fortunate, however, and simply found yourself panicking at the deep end and trying to keep afloat, you will remember that feeling of knowing there was information you needed, but not being sure about what nor whom to ask.

Effective induction is essential to the performance of your team, and one of your required functions as a team leader – even if you're a first-line leader – is to provide an induction for new members of your team. If the college provides an institutional induction for newly appointed staff, you will nevertheless still need to ensure a programme of induction is organised and implemented which will introduce the newcomer to the team, subject, section, school or whatever area your leadership covers. And you will need to evaluate the effectiveness of that induction in order to ensure that you are providing the necessary support. Here we arrive back again at a familiar diagram in Figure 6.3: the team leader's mantra of quality assurance.

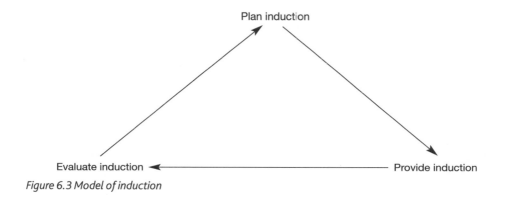

Figure 6.3 Model of induction

2. Monitoring performance

Monitoring the performance of your team is an essential part of a leader's quality assurance role. Today there are clear benchmarks to help you evaluate team members' performance in the form of national standards (SVUK, 2006), but the manner in which you carry out this aspect of your leadership role may be crucial to your aim of winning the hearts and minds of your team. In order that such monitoring should be seen as supportive rather than interpreted as a form of 'surveillance' (Usher and Edwards, 1994), as team leader you will need to distinguish very firmly between supportive monitoring and 'surveillance':

SUPPORTIVE MONITORING	'SURVEILLANCE'
Negotiating place and time for observation	Dictating place and time, or making 'surprise' visit for observation
Discussing performance	Judging performance
Negotiating points for action	Dictating points for action
Finding aspects to praise	Focusing on aspects to criticise

3. Communication

Effective induction and monitoring both depend on a wider set of skills which we usually refer to as 'communication'. They are the skills which enable us to interact positively with others – to connect with people – and we looked at these in some detail in Chapter 2. Indeed, every aspect of supporting the professional development of individuals is heavily dependent on our ability, and willingness, to generate trust, share information, listen and treat others with respect and courtesy. Individuals will be more likely to gain full benefit from professional development activities if they are led rather than driven to them.

4. Agreeing achievable, measurable, specific objectives

Perhaps the most important word here is 'agreeing'. For individuals to feel a sense of ownership about their professional action plan, these need to be arrived at by a process of negotiation. Such negotiation in itself can encourage members of your team to engage in reflective practice, as we saw earlier when we focused on coaching and mentoring. The objectives agreed need to be specific and achievable, and you may find yourself having to give some guidance on exactly what this means. If we take Maya's unsuccessful encounter with Doug as an example, she was able to identify two very specific objectives:

- how to set out a lesson plan (*It'd be really useful if I could have look at how you set out your lesson plans*);
- how to incorporate differentiation into her lesson plans (*I can't get my head around this thing about differentiation*).

Unfortunately, Doug wasn't able to help her to formalise these as part of a professional action plan because he was too busy trying to gloss over the fact that he wasn't meeting these particular elements of the standards himself. But nevertheless, they are specific, achievable and measurable, so that a more effective team leader would be able to monitor Maya's progress against them and give her clear feedback – formative feedback – as she works towards the objectives and summative, positive feedback when she has achieved them. But what if she had said something like this?

Maya: *I just want to be a really brilliant teacher. I just want to inspire people. I want to do really good lessons and I want all the learners to think I'm the coolest teacher ever.*

This is where the team leader needs to give some solid guidance about what these ambitions might mean in terms of observable objectives. And, of course, what they're probably going to mean in the first place is exactly the same thing: getting to grips with lesson planning!

5. Negotiate support

As well as the objectives for professional development, it will also be necessary to negotiate the nature and degree of support the individual will need in order to achieve them. Doug probably wouldn't understand this, because part of what we're talking about here is differentiation. One individual might ask for – and need – a great deal of direct support. Another might ask for – and need – very little. Where you will really need to bring your negotiation and leadership skills into play is in facilitating the support for those who insist they need very little but in fact require a lot.

6. Review outcomes against goals and give constructive feedback

Having negotiated and agreed the individual team member's development objectives and the support necessary to help achieve them, you'll then need to engage in a regular review of progress. This will necessitate giving clear and constructive feedback. The skills involved here are again those which are central to the processes of mentoring and coaching, and so let's go back again to Gordon and Maya and see what happened in the course of their second meeting.

Gordon	*Is this the lesson plan? Thanks. So how did you feel the lesson went?*
Maya	*Not too bad. I didn't get the timings quite right. But the differentiated activities seemed to work really well.*
Gordon	*This is a very clearly drawn up lesson plan. Lots of changes of activity – just the thing to keep these learners interested and on task. How did you find twenty minutes worked for questions and answers?*
Maya	*Way, way too long!*
Gordon	*That's the sort of thing you learn with practice. And you've learnt it now. And you've made a really good start here. Well done.*

Notice that Gordon begins by asking for Maya's view. And, while he acknowledges that she got something wrong, he ensures that this is presented constructively, and he also makes sure he gives her praise where it's due. This may all sound very simple and obvious. But in the course of a busy and stressful working day, these positive, productive ways of interacting can be easily lost. As an effective team leader you will, of course, always keep them in mind.

Supporting professional development of teams

We've now discussed at some length the development of individual team members. But what of teams as a whole? Well, all the skills and strategies that go to make you successful in supporting one team member will prove just as useful in supporting the development of your team as a whole. There are, however, some additional issues to bear in mind. For example, where for individuals you can provide one-to-one mentoring, with whole-team development you will need to:

- identify development priorities within the team as a whole;
- design and contribute to team training and development events;
- rigorously evaluate such team training and development ;
- ensure that all team members have access to the training and development provided.

You will find all of these identified in the National Occupational Standards for Leadership and Management.

The 'dark side'

Being over-directive, too judgemental, pushing people too hard, expecting too much or too little – these would be symptomatic of the dark side, as would an intolerance of difference and an obsession with rigidly standardised operating methods. So, too, would be having 'favourites' and developing some members of your team while neglecting to support others.

As leaders, we often get the staff we deserve, and, as followers, we can end up with the leaders we deserve too. What do we mean by this? Well, just as our assumptions about our students have been shown to drastically affect the way we behave towards them and thereby their subsequent performance, so it is with leaders. This has been called the 'Pygmalion Effect'. In Shaw's play, Eliza would always be a flower-girl to Professor Higgins because he always treated her like one (Bennis, 1989). How well the people we lead perform is, likewise, determined to a frightening extent by what we expect of them. Treat a potential leader like they need constant supervision and detailed instructions and they will generally reward you by becoming dependent and lacking in initiative. Recent research has dubbed this the 'Set-up to Fail Syndrome', (Manzoni and Barsoux, 2002). But leaders can break this self-fulfilling prophesy cycle by trying to avoid stereotyping, talking openly to staff about whether they feel they have enough freedom and responsibility, and, importantly, actively encouraging feedback and mentoring by colleagues from another department, to ensure team members are exposed to alternative, and perhaps more objective, review processes.

Issues for the Lifelong Learning sector

The theme of creating capability raises an important question for leadership teams in the sector. What is it that their particular institution requires in these unpredictable and rapidly changing times? Is it strong leadership, defined as clear direction, top-down strategic planning and an experienced and able top team, capable of steering the organisation through radical change and tough choices? Or, alternatively, is the prime function of the leadership team to ensure that the capability is there, throughout the organisation, to learn and adapt to changing demands, and continue identifying and developing talent into the future? There has been much discussion about the suitability of 'distributed' forms of leadership to lifelong learning institutions (Lumby et al., 2005), and many of the leaders we spoke to felt that their colleges had reached the point where the key role of leaders was doing just this: creating long-term capability by developing leadership at every level in the organisation. And yet some of the same leaders readily acknowledged that they had also gone through periods of enormous upheaval not so long before, where a far more directive and instrumental leadership style had seemed unavoidable. Of course, ultimately leaders need to provide both clear direction from the top and the organisation-wide capability to develop and adapt. However, the emphasis may depend on the evolution of the particular institution and the circumstances in which it finds itself.

Self-evaluation and development

Consider now the support and development needs of your own team. How did you go about identifying these? How often do you coach team members? Do you act as mentor to people outside your immediate team? When did you last provide an opportunity for one of your team to undertake a project that would stretch their capabilities? What support did you put in place? Think about each of your team. Do you treat them differently, and how much of this is down to legitimate reasons of personality or preference? Could you take more of a risk with delegating tasks? Are there those 'safe pairs of hands' whom you may have found it easier just to rely on instead of really challenging them? How large a part does negotiation play in establishing individuals' developmental goals?

Is there anything about this aspect of your leadership role that you would like to change, having worked through this chapter?

Summary of key points

In this chapter we have:

- examined the importance of modelling good practice and communicating organisational values;
- considered ways in which teams and individuals can be supported in their professional development, such as mentoring and coaching;
- explored strategies for assessing the effectiveness of teams and individuals;
- considered the importance of providing a 'crucible' for the growth of new leaders;
- applied strategies from earlier chapters to building and maintaining productive working relationships;
- explored some of the issues surrounding leadership succession;
- provided opportunities for you to identify areas in which your own team needs support and development.

7. Making things happen

Introduction

So far in this book, we have talked a lot about the way in which leaders read situations, form relationships, communicate and learn. Amid all of this thought-provoking material on motivating, inspiring and developing people, we must not forget that leaders are also expected to deliver results. The nature of their leadership role and their position in the organisation may affect what kind of action they personally take. But all leaders will be expected to make things happen, to turn that compelling story into reality.

This is what we look for from our leaders, is it not? We want to be reassured that they are in control and will direct us to where we need to go. Or is this only part of the picture? Surely we also want our leaders to delegate, to give us responsibility and involve us in determining what happens to our organisation and how it delivers its objectives. It is fair to say that most of us, as followers, want it all and on a stick. We want organisation and direction as well as empowerment, responsibility and involvement. We want consultation, but get impatient if this does not result in a decision and some action. As team members, we have a need to feel affiliated with group objectives as well as a need to assert our own beliefs (Kets de Vries, 2001). Yes, it is tough at the top.

This is not mere sophistry. There is a fondness currently for debates within the Lifelong Learning sector about moving from transactional to transformational and distributed models of leadership (Bennett et al., 2003; Lumby et al., 2005). At the same time there are concerns about the apparent conflict between this and a perceived impetus for greater performativity and accountability (Jameson, 2006). Striking this balance effectively has got to be a key challenge for any leader in this sector.

Our own conversations with leaders in FE reinforced this idea that successful leaders make things happen. They fix blockages to change and development, they secure resources, they confront long-standing problems, and they can generally point to a whole host of examples where ideas have been turned into action through their impetus, support and persistence. They emphasise the increasing importance of sound data, especially financial data, and the need for robust systems and processes to ensure that plans are kept on track and remain commercially viable. But people also need to feel accountable. Success for most institutions, therefore, depends on as many people as possible feeling as though they are able to take decisions and make things happen *themselves*.

The Leadership and Management Standards provide some guidance on *How* a leader *makes effective decisions and solves problems*. They also include '*displays confidence, courage, stamina and tenacity*' among the interpersonal abilities required for confronting issues and handling critical incidents (LLUK, 2005). But the importance to the leader's role of making things happen is perhaps best demonstrated by the fact that elements appear in all four of the key outcomes.

A	Develop Strategic Practice	A3.1	Implement strategic plan
B	Develop and Sustain Learning	B1.2	Implement an operational plan
		B1.3	Monitor and review progress
		B3.2	Ensure efficient and effective deployment of staff resources
C	Lead Teams and Individuals	C1.1	Manage self
		C3.2	Deal professionally with conflict
D	Manage Finance and Resources	D1.2	Secure approval for expenditure
		D2	Manage finance
		D3	Manage physical resources

So, in this chapter we shall be addressing the following questions about turning vision and mission into action.

- In ensuring that things get done, how do we achieve the correct balance between controlling and enabling people?
- What sorts of things do successful leaders do to ensure that ideas are turned into productive action?
- How can we get better at confronting issues and handling conflict?
- What is the connection between taking action and learning?
- What happens if our bias to action is not informed by a strong set of values?
- How can we develop our own preferred way of making things happen?

Freedom or control?

Nothing like starting with the easy questions, is there? Conscious that this is a topic debated throughout the ages by philosophers and politicians alike, we will confine our thoughts to specifics. Consider the following.

TASK

If you were given the job of improving the quality of teaching in your particular organisation, an issue no doubt very close to the hearts of a few institutions and arguably a legitimate continuing aim for all, how would you go about it? Once you have jotted down some ideas, try classifying them under two headings. One contains all those changes that are about standards, or inspection, or self-assessment, or appraisal processes – in other words things that create structure and limitations. We'll call that column 'Control'. Under the other heading put all those ideas which are to do with developing skills, giving more responsibility, motivating and inspiring – in other words things that remove constraints. We'll call that column 'Freedom'. What kind of balance have you ended up with?

Could this be what some commentators have referred to as the distinction between leadership and management? Management is seen as administration, systems, structure, control and maintaining the status quo. Leadership, on the other hand, is about innovation, development, inspiring trust and taking the long view (Bennis, 1989). Such a distinction would identify the activities under your 'Control' column as features of 'management', whereas the activities like developing, motivating and inspiring would sound more like 'leadership'. How happy are you with this distinction, and what would you conclude about whether people prefer to be well managed or well led?.

DISCUSSION

Our own inclination is to see management as an integral part of leadership. To make management and leadership appear mutually exclusive is to devalue the vital importance of sound execution and delivery. It is more helpful to see these two activities as complementary parts of a single role, at whatever level it is practised (Kotter, 1996). People need to be well managed and well led. If either one of these elements is weak or missing, then people can find it very stressful.

So, as followers, we need not only structure and a sense of progress, but also some control over the work we do. Good teachers can inspire students and motivate them to achieve to their full potential. But they can only really begin to do this once the classroom is reasonably under control. As 'amateur' visitors to the job of teaching soon discover, classroom management is a pre-requisite of all the sexy, you-transformed-my-life-sir/miss Mr Chips stuff, and it is a complex and valuable skill in its own right.

The idea of leadership without management is epitomised by the, perhaps apocryphal, report on a young army officer which read:

> *His men will follow him anywhere, if only out of a sense of curiosity . . .*
> (Lygo, 1996)

Squaring the circle

So what have others to say about this balancing act? Some years ago, John Adair drew partly on his own experience of leadership training in the military to develop Action Centred Leadership, an approach to leadership development based around his three circles model. This presents leadership as being concerned with three interconnecting needs:

- the needs of the individual member of the team;
- the needs of the team as a whole; and
- the demands of the task.

Effective leaders balance these three elements in getting things done, ensuring that individuals are trained, appraised and given the freedom to act, that the team is composed of the right people, properly briefed and encouraged to work together towards a common goal, and that the task is properly understood and broken down into key objectives, with success measures and deadlines (Adair, 1983).

Each of the elements must be seen in relation to the other two, and if any one is neglected then the whole is undermined. So if, as section leader, you focus on hitting your targets at the expense of developing your staff, then their motivation suffers, the team becomes dysfunctional and the task (i.e. targets) suffer. Similarly, if you nurture your team, but lose sight of the task, then the team will lose heart and individuals will not have the opportunity to stretch themselves and grow (Wallace and Gravells, 2006).

This emphasis on teams and collaboration is echoed elsewhere in trying to describe the difference between previous 'command and control' approaches to leadership and the challenge faced by modern leaders, grappling with different expectations on the part of their teams. Rupert Eales-White sees a transition from fixed hierarchies with controlling leaders in charge of every decision, getting their way through force of personality, argument or status, towards more distributed decision-making, where the leader's main role is to create an environment in which people can collaborate effectively to make things happen on their own initiative. This can be summarised as in Figure 7.1.

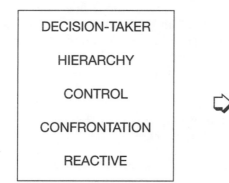

Figure 7.1 Hierarchies to distributed decision-making
(adapted from Eales-White, 1992)

During the 1990s an international research project involving over 1,450 managers identified the five most important leadership capabilities for the future. Two of them were *Empowerment and Producing results* (the others were *Visioning, Leading change and Customer focus*) (Ready, 1993; van Maurik, 2001). As well as providing meaning and direction, act and get results is one of the things leaders do (Bennis and Powell, 2000).

How do leaders help others to be more effective?

Part of the answer to this question lies in developing people and growing future leaders which we covered in Chapters 5 and 6. However, there are other, perhaps more transactional, practices which help leaders generate action themselves and on the part of others.

Get yourself organised

The first thing to say is that we will find it difficult, if not impossible, to organise others if we are incapable of organising ourselves. Covey sees the first steps in becoming more effective as being those that help us to achieve *self-mastery* (Covey, 1989). The *public victories*, involving teamwork and collaboration, come after. Until we have learned the disciplines of being clear about what we are setting out to achieve, taking responsibility for what happens in our lives and ensuring that we focus on what is most important, we will struggle to help others to do this.

Try developing your own ways of remembering tasks, setting priorities and avoiding wasteful activity. Here are some ideas.

- Ask yourself what you are here for. What is the point of your job? Without an overall *purpose*, *decisions* about priorities and objectives are built on sand.
- Agree *objectives*. Try to make these objectives SMART (see below).
- Separate *building* tasks from *maintenance* tasks. *Building* tasks help you to achieve your overall purpose and objectives. *Maintenance* tasks are the million things we have to respond to every day to keep things running.
- Categorise activities by *urgency* and *importance* and then plan your time. *Urgent* tasks must be done quickly but may or may not be important. *Important* tasks are those that contribute to your purpose and objectives and therefore deserve to have more time spent on them. (Adapted from Wallace and Gravells, 2006.)

Having got their own house in order, how do effective leaders help others to deliver? This is partly a mindset and partly a question of hard work. Leaders need to believe that they can shape their own lives (a challenge in itself, perhaps, for a sector heavily influenced by government intervention), but they also need to apply the requisite techniques to help people turn ideas into results. This is what Collins calls a *culture of discipline* (Collins, 2001).

One way of studying these techniques is to watch a good project manager in action. Here are some of the things we might see them doing.

- *Be clear about what you are trying to achieve.* You may have run across the term SMART objectives. The acronym stands for Specific, Measurable, Agreed, Realistic and Time-bound. When setting out to make things happen, it helps to be absolutely clear *what* it is you want to happen. That way, your team will feel more able to take the right decisions, without asking you.

- Set *milestones.* Break your actions down into milestones with defined success measures. Try to be clear what success will look like. This is not always easy and may not be measurable in any quantitative way, but achieving these 'mini-goals' can be hugely motivating and reassuring for you and the team, and they help you to see if you are on track. This process can also help you to anticipate probable difficulties and think of contingency plans.

- *Secure resources.* Larger-scale actions may require funding or extra pairs of hands or particular pieces of equipment. How best can these be obtained? Is some horse-trading required with other departments? Your team will only feel able to take the initiative if they have the resources to do so.

- *Look at the data.* Yes, some people can become a bit obsessive about measurement and numbers, just as some people are scared to death of them. An important part of leadership is knowing when you have all the information you are going to get and it is time to go with your instinct. Nevertheless, schools and colleges are big organisations with large budgets and are expected to run on commercial lines. One thing was clear from our conversations with leaders in FE: these days ensuring that you have the systems in place to provide timely performance data, and understanding what this data is telling you, is increasingly essential for leaders in Lifelong Learning. Without it you could be tackling the wrong problem in the first place, or working your socks off without seeing any progress.

  There are various methods for reporting data in a way that gives you and the team an easily understood snapshot of what is going on. Some record key measures on a performance 'dashboard' which echoes the kind of display you get in a vehicle. Others use a 'balanced scorecard' to ensure they take a number of perspectives into account and measure a variety of 'soft' and 'hard' performance indicators (Kaplan and Norton, 1993). Another variation on the same theme is to identify 'critical success factors', things that have to be achieved for the action plan to succeed.

- *Set up robust communications.* Who is affected by the action you are taking? Who can help? Who might actively get in the way? Good leaders have a strategy for talking to all of these people, as well as for keeping the team informed of progress or setbacks. Communication may take the form of regular meetings, reports, e-mails, newsletters or telephone conversations, just so long as it is relevant to the task. One idea is to structure reporting around the SMART objectives. This soon reveals where time is being wasted on less useful activity.

- *Track progress.* This is obviously easier if you have clear objectives and milestones and you have robust communications in place. Encourage the team to report proactively on progress, but be clear you will chase if necessary. Then it is down to ensuring feedback on progress/performance is regularly reviewed and any issues identified. Effective leaders are often flexible about *how* people do things provided they deliver the right result.

- *Take corrective action.* Back to the whole theme of this chapter. Clear objectives and regular monitoring are of little use unless the leader is diligent in ensuring that any deviation from expected progress is addressed. This is not just about 'whip-cracking', although there may be some of that. It is primarily about joint problem-solving. Meetings and individual conversations need to end with actions in somebody's hands, not problems on a flip chart.

Of course, when great leaders implement actions, they do all this and more, including all of the kinds of behaviour we refer to in other chapters. But the list above is a good start. To learn more, read one of the many good books on project management.

When technique is just not enough

So, is making things happen just a matter of getting the techniques down 'pat' and being a good project manager? Well, no, because this is about encouraging a state of mind, not just a collection of behaviours. Excellent leaders have a 'bias to action', they want to 'sort things out'. They are energised by the idea of confronting issues of performance or resources (Jameson, 2006). This is not about being pugnacious, but about an intolerance of 'success preventers'. Leaders can vary in their approach to this, from the low-profile but quietly persistent stickler for high standards to the more overtly confrontational character who uses very public and symbolic gestures to draw metaphorical 'lines in the sand'. Different circumstances may favour different styles, but what they all have in common is a willingness to fix those 'success preventers' and not back off from the conflict this might cause.

Using as a case study Bill Bratton, the man credited with bringing down New York's spiralling crime rate in the early 1990s, Kim and Mauborgne identify four hurdles which have to be addressed as part of what they call *tipping point leadership* (Kim and Mauborgne, 2003).

- *Cognitive hurdle.* Leaders must get agreement on the scale of the problem and the need for action. This may take more than data. Bratton made (presumably terrified) senior managers ride the subway to see first-hand what their customers were experiencing.

- *Resource hurdle.* Leaders know how to build momentum for action without extra resources, by focusing existing resources on what is likely to generate the biggest return. Bratton reduced arrest-processing time from 16 hours to one by introducing mobile 'bust buses', or arrest-processing centres around the corner from targeted subway stations.

- *Motivational hurdle.* Leaders do not just help people recognise what action is needed, they encourage them to want to take it. This is about framing the challenge in ways that make it appear more achievable, and about making personal accountability for progress clear. Bratton focused on spotlighting key influencers and requiring them to publicly report progress, as well as breaking the turnaround challenge into local goals, district by district.

- *Political hurdle.* Leaders understand the reality of organisational politics and ensure that they have key stakeholders 'on side' before they attempt to confront long-standing problems. They also understand the benefits of communicating directly with those whose responses matter most. Bratton gained several key allies, including the mayor, Rudolph Giuliani, and made his case directly to the press, ensuring that public opinion heard his calls for action accurately. For middle managers in Lifelong Learning institutions this is a particular challenge, as they are often forced to act as mediators between the senior team and staff (Briggs, 2001).

This desire to face up to and overcome hurdles is reinforced in great leaders by the positive way in which they respond to setbacks, a theme we explore further in Chapter 8. Tackling performance issues begins with facing up to hard truths about your team or organisation (Heifetz and Laurie, 2001). It means subscribing publicly to certain standards of behaviour and remaining strong and determined in tackling those who ignore them, whether this be as trivial as dress code and turning up to meetings on time, or as serious as bullying and discrimination.

Handling conflict

All this is tricky, to say the least, if the leader is fixated on not upsetting anyone. Strangely, however, it is equally problematic for many leaders who relish conflict. For this is not about belligerence. Aggressive leaders are often bullies, and rarely seek 'win–win' solutions that allow both sides to benefit. Their aim is to win at all costs, and the cost is all too often the support and respect of those who work for them.

Excellent leaders view conflict not as right and wrong, but as a reflection of different perspectives on reality within the organisation (Bennett et al., 2003). Rather than despairing at the prospect of another difference of opinion, they see a chance for ideas and values to be challenged, an opportunity to better understand another perspective on the problem – in short, a positive force for learning and improvement. Working in education, we should find this frame of mind easier than most. (Of course, as teachers, we may just be too used to being right all the time!)

TASK

Let's go back now to a scenario we first encountered in Chapter 5. Jean, the Head of Faculty, is having trouble with two of her Heads of School. If you remember, we left her reflecting on how best to deal with the situation. Here's a reminder of the challenge she's facing.

> Two of her Heads of School simply do not get on. The animosity between them flares up frequently at Faculty Management Group (FMG) meetings. It seems that whatever line Orson takes, Lilly will take the opposite. Their heated exchanges at these meetings make everyone uncomfortable and often threaten to turn into full-scale shouting matches. The situation is further complicated by the fact that Jean finds it difficult to remain impartial. Orson and his wife are personal friends of hers, and Orson is always a very supportive colleague. He is also popular with his team, and his School is well run. On the other hand, Lilly has an abrasive manner and she's made some decisions recently which raise questions about her judgement. Moreover, the staff in Lilly's School appear generally miserable and demotivated. With an OFSTED inspection coming up, Jean fears that inspectors will arrive to find:

1. An FMG which can't agree decisions.

2. A Head of School whose decision-making is flawed.

3. A School full of unhappy staff, which is probably having an impact on learners' motivation.

4. An ongoing atmosphere of tension and conflict within the Faculty.

Imagine you were in a position to advise Jean on this. She has reflected on the situation, but is now also seeking your advice. Consider the following questions:

1. What are the issues?

2. What are Jean's options?

3. What action would you advise her to take, and why?

4. How should she go about it?

5. What skills and qualities will she need to succeed?

In tackling this exercise, you may want to remind yourself of some of the 'connecting with people' skills we covered in Chapter 2.

DISCUSSION

If leaders accept conflict as an inevitable and positive force for change, this allows them to focus on how best to manage it. Successful strategies that Jean might follow could include some of the following.

- *Establishing common ground at the start.* Look at what issues unite Orson and Lilly, not what separates them.

- *Separating personalities from the real problem.* Help her two Heads of School to focus on what the real issues are by identifying and isolating the personality-driven causes of friction.

- *Encouraging 'constructive conflict'.* Teach Orson and Lilly to seek information about the other's views, while showing respect for the individual, tempering advocacy with enquiry, and genuinely seeking to understand the other point of view.

- *Exploring feelings as well as facts.* Help these two articulate how they feel about each other and why. Coach them in recognising how this is affecting their behaviour and how they might control it.

- *Establishing people's needs, rather than dwelling on negotiating positions.* Demand that Lilly and Orson express what they want from each other in a constructive and assertive way.

- *Gaining acceptance that disagreements are a group responsibility.* Do not allow individual team members to escape their responsibility for managing this conflict more positively.

- *Encouraging joint problem-solving.* Help these individuals to seek and find opportunities for mutual benefit.

- *Bearing in mind that she may need to adjust her own view,* Jean must not lose sight of how she may herself be contributing to the problem through her own behaviour. (How might she be doing this?)

(Adapted from Bolman and Deal, 1991; West, 1994.)

Such approaches may feel counter-intuitive in a society whose institutions, political and legal, are based on principles of argument and counter-argument and combative debate. However, there are those who feel strongly that being able to see and understand several perspectives in parallel, and thereby foster collaboration out of conflict, ultimately achieves better solutions. This is the theory on which Edward de Bono's 'six thinking hats' approach is based (de Bono, 1985).

Taking action and learning

The idea of conflict as an opportunity for improvement brings us neatly to perhaps the most important reason that leaders need to ensure that vision is translated into action. Action helps us learn faster. Whether it is the right action or the wrong one, we still benefit because we can learn from mistakes as well as success. The old adage about those who never made mistakes never making anything has a lot of truth to it. Research suggests that most leaders, in fact, learn their craft largely from experience, often during times of great hardship (Conger, 2004). As professional educators we understand the learning power of trying something out, doing it for ourselves, rather than just being told about it. Collins and Porras urge leaders to *try a lot of stuff and keep what works* (Collins and Porras, 1994). Yet when it comes to leading others we can sometimes forget this simple truth. We wait and wait until something is perfectly planned (we may wait for ever), or we have all the data we want (which rarely happens), or until the time is just right (it never is).

Equally, we may be too quick to criticise failure in others, searching for scapegoats instead of trying to create an environment in which experimentation and mistakes are, within reason, accepted as part of learning and innovation. (For more on this see Chapters 5 and 6.)

The 'dark side'

What might we see, then, when leaders try to make things happen without some underpinning values, when the balance between control and freedom, which we talked about at the start of this chapter, is uneven? Well, an obvious result would be the worst excesses of 'macho' management. In trying to force actions through by sheer authority or 'diktat', the leader takes away people's control over their work, demotivates them and, at worst, is reduced to bullying and browbeating to get their own way. The result of such autocratic leadership is often a team or organisation in which stress levels and staff turnover are alarmingly high, but creativity and innovation are depressingly low.

The other inevitable result of actions being determined only by the few is that there is no check on individual versus organisational priorities. This can affect not only the quality of the thinking, but also the probity of the outcome. How much easier is it for motives of personal gain and ambition to dominate the issues that are addressed when one person, or a leadership elite, is calling all the shots?

Issues for the Lifelong Learning sector

It is perhaps a fear of this kind of control, or the lessons of the recent past, that inclines the Lifelong Learning sector to look for some accommodation between what it regards as academic and managerial leadership approaches. However much more formal performance management may have been introduced into the job in recent years, the classroom teacher is still a much more autonomous role than some, and it might be argued that looser forms of control, more collegiate styles of leadership and greater empowerment are the most likely to meet with success. And yet many would argue that the job of leaders in Lifelong Learning is becoming more and more outcomes-focused.

The challenge facing leaders in the sector is how to demonstrate results and effect the sheer pace of change being demanded by some, while trying to adopt more transformational and distributed leadership approaches. How do you make things happen even more quickly while keeping staff engaged? The answer lies not in throwing out the transactional 'baby' with the command and control 'bathwater'. Leaders must find ways of encouraging people to take responsibility and engaging them in creating a motivating vision of the future, while getting even smarter at transactional management and execution.

Self-evaluation and development

How would you currently rate *your* ability to make things happen? Is this achieved by creating the SMART objectives, regular feedback, support and sense of accountability that makes it easier for your team to take positive action? Or is it at least partly achieved by dint of working long hours clearing up other people's mess and 'doing it yourself because otherwise it won't get done'? Are you someone who produces a result on time, even if it is not your best work, or are you more inclined to miss the odd deadline or 'forget' certain tasks altogether in the interests of coming up with a truly excellent and innovative approach?

If there is a thorny issue lingering on your 'to do' list that just refuses to go away, however much you ignore it, ask yourself what is stopping you confronting it. Is it resources? An unwillingness to delegate? The fear that you will upset someone? Or just anxiety about making a hash of it? Go back and read the section on conflict. Could you reframe this as an opportunity? How will you become better at confronting these sorts of issue if you do not take action? (On the other hand, maybe you do not even have a 'to do' list?!)

One way of analysing your natural leadership approach to getting things done is to use Blanchard's Situational Leadership Model (Blanchard et al.,1986). In his model, the leadership approach is defined by the degree of control versus the degree of support. This gives four leadership styles, which good leaders can move between according to the demands of the situation and the individual. Which would be your natural style?

- *Directive* – high control but low support. The leader gives detailed instructions which are not for debate and expects them to be followed.
- *Coaching* – high control and lots of support too. The leader still tells people the task and the way to do it, but also offers to help and coach them in achieving it.
- *Supporting* – low control but high support. The leader trusts the person's ability to achieve the task with little direction, but they are ready to jump in and provide additional help.
- *Delegating* – low in control and support. The leader has enough confidence in people's experience and reliability to simply 'agree and forget'.

(Adapted from Wallace and Gravells, 2006.)

Whatever your assessment, as we indicated earlier, a good place to start your self-development is with your own personal organisation. Take another look at the section on self-organisation. How many of these disciplines do *you* apply?

Once you feel that you have got yourself organised, then you can think about how you organise others and some of the project management disciplines mentioned earlier. If this is not a strength for you, how about persuading your boss to give you a small project to lead? Is there anyone among your colleagues whose project management skills you admire? Could they mentor you?

But what if you are a congenitally disorganised (albeit hugely charismatic and inspirational!) leader? Well, you may have to think seriously about who can help you. After all, asking for help is a way of taking action too. Maybe you need someone on the team who can openly act as your 'organiser', keep you on track and ensure loose ends are tied up. Of course, you will have to empower them to do this, and it does not absolve you of the obligation to keep learning and improving.

Summary of key points

- Excellent leaders ensure that their own actions are informed by clear purpose, objectives and priorities.
- They use structure and planning disciplines to create an environment in which others can make decisions and take action confidently.
- They have a desire to overcome obstacles and they seek ways of making this an achievable priority for others.
- They regard conflict as a positive force for change and improvement and find ways of confronting and managing it.

Above all, great leaders appreciate that people, including themselves, learn by doing, and must therefore feel able to take action without an overwhelming fear of getting it wrong.

CHAPTER OBJECTIVES

This chapter is designed to help you to:

- consider the impact your response to obstacles has on your effectiveness as a leader;

- explore ways in which to generate a positive attitude in yourself and others;

- balance the need to protect your team and at the same time support them in facing reality;

- evaluate your own strengths and development needs.

Introduction

Remember those films about underdog sports teams getting to the big competition and about to be crushed in the final scene? Or the soldiers trapped in the foxhole, overwhelmingly outnumbered? Or perhaps it was the group of kids about to put on a show in the local warehouse/garage/shed, only to have it demolished by the wicked property developer? Whatever the scenario, you can bet that the coach/sergeant/ringleader, when they looked into camera with shining eyes, did not say, 'Oh b*****ks to this! We're completely stuffed. Let's all go down the pub and complain about it over few beers.'

Successful leaders seem to have the resilience to remain positive in spite of setbacks and to inspire a sense of hope and optimism in others. Leaders in Lifelong Learning may not have to deal with enemy soldiers or wicked property developers (OK well maybe), but they are nevertheless prey to any number of internal and external forces, some helpful, some not. How we respond to these challenges can make a big difference to how effective we are as leaders.

You may feel that you have little or no control over some of these forces, but you do have control over how you respond. You can choose to despair, be it about government intervention, the local economy or funding cutbacks. It is a tempting reaction, especially if you feel that you are battling against the odds to create positive change, as many leaders in the sector no doubt do. But in reacting this way, you will almost certainly transmit your pessimism to those you lead, sapping their energy and will in the process.

So do you take all of this anxiety upon yourself while smiling and joking through the working day, protecting your team from the harsh realities of life like a human shield? Well, that hardly seems sustainable either. Apart from being patronising and disempowering to your staff, it is likely to land you in hospital. And yet the leaders we spoke to in FE seemed to have found a way of facing up to obstacles and staying positive. They could fight battles, argue their corner, but recognise when it was time to move on and do what they had to do. Furthermore, they could retain the energy and motivation to try to do it better than anyone else and generate the same positive energy in others.

The Leadership and Management Standards contain little *explicit* reference to this aspect of leadership, although they do indicate that an effective leader *displays confidence, courage, stamina and tenacity*, (LLUK, 2005). However, the need to stay positive is implicit in virtually all of the elements of the Lifelong Learning UK model, from leading and managing change (A3) to maintaining a healthy working environment (B2.3).

So, in this chapter we shall be addressing the following questions about staying positive:

- How do effective leaders cope with obstacles and setbacks that are outside of their control?
- To what extent should leaders 'shield' their followers from bad news?
- What do leaders do to ensure that people remain focused and motivated during tough challenges?
- What happens when staying positive is divorced from any set of values or ethics?
- How can leaders find their own ways of staying positive?

Make your own luck

In his book *The luck factor*, psychologist Richard Wiseman draws on extensive research with people who consider themselves lucky or unlucky. He makes some interesting observations about human behaviour and how it affects success (Wiseman, 2003). He suggests that four categories of behaviour are the real reason behind people's good fortune, and that feeling lucky is something of a self-fulfilling prophecy.

- *Maximise opportunities.* 'Lucky' people develop and maintain strong support networks. They tend to remain relaxed about life and therefore open to new experiences. This means more opportunities come their way.
- *Follow your hunches.* 'Lucky' people listen to their instincts and keep an open mind about using intuition as well as rational thinking. (Remember we talked earlier about an instinct for opportunity?) They will go with their gut, and exploit opportunities that others might miss.
- *Expect to be lucky.* 'Lucky' people tend to be optimistic. This makes them persevere in the face of hardship, expecting a positive outcome. They enter into situations confident of success, and this affects people's perception of them and therefore how positively they respond.

- *Convert misfortune into success.* Finally, 'lucky' people refuse to dwell on mishaps. Their positive outlook enables them to see these as temporary at worst and quickly move on to potential 'upsides'. This gives them the energy and determination to press on and snatch victory from the jaws of defeat.

Doubtless, there is something of a circular argument here. Given these characteristics, are 'lucky' people simply presenting themselves as fortunate, while getting as big a kicking as everyone else? Whatever the logic, it does not undermine the point we wish to make about effective leaders. As followers, we all know that we are motivated and inspired by those who give us faith and hope, a sense that we have choices rather than dead ends. This is not born out of a foolish optimism on their part that they can change the world or that everything they touch is transformed into gold. On the contrary, these leaders, like the ones we spoke to in FE, are actually able to be very clear about what they can change and what has moved beyond their *circle of influence* (Covey, 1989). They concentrate on the things they can do something about. This is what enables them to avoid wasteful breast-beating about this new initiative or that withdrawal of funding, and focus clearly on where they are able to make an impact.

It is not about being a pushover either. We spoke to people who have lobbied long and hard at national level for and against decisions about which they felt passionately. The point is that they knew how to recognise when they could no longer control the outcome and needed to move on. Such a positive approach to adversity not only preserves their own sanity and helps them to deliver success against the odds, it also spurs on their teams. As a principal pointed out to us, leaders are watched very closely, whether they like it or not. The people in their teams are acutely sensitive to changes of mood and demeanour. If the boss looks hangdog and depressed, let alone talks in terms of defeat, then we really start to worry about our future.

An excellent example of a leader who demonstrated this positive approach is Ernest Shackleton. Of course, you'll probably not often be called upon to lead your team through icy wastes and South Atlantic storms (though, given the increasing rate of change and reform in FE, who knows?) but his is a useful story for any leader to keep in mind. Indeed, he is often cited these days (for example, Morrell and Capparell, 2001) as an iconic example of positive leadership in the face of adversity, having successfully ensured the survival and safe return of every member of his crew, despite a series of disasters which included their ship being crushed by ice and the entire expedition being marooned on the shifting ice floes of the Antarctic. Was it luck? Well, in Wiseman's sense, yes, it was. Shackleton *maximised opportunities*; he remained calm and relaxed, and presented the predicament to his men as an opportunity to demonstrate their courage and to fulfil their appetite for adventure. He *followed his hunches*, setting out in an open boat to fetch help across 2,000 miles of South Atlantic Ocean – a feat many would have thought impossible. He *remained optimistic*, and encouraged optimism in his crew, speaking to them always in terms of positive outcomes and the certainty of survival. And, of course, he *converted* that disastrous *misfortune* of a wrecked expedition *into a success story* of survival and courage. As he wrote to his wife, *Not a man lost, and we have been through Hell.* We think of Shackleton as a great leader not only because he was able to make his own 'luck', but also because throughout the hardships of that 1914–16 expedition, he secured the survival of his entire team.

Guardian angel or ghost of future yet to come?

Does this mean that leaders protect us from the outside world, keeping us positive by painting a rosier picture than is really justified? We can see how leaders in Lifelong Learning mediate between government, the local community and the college, or senior management and staff, depending on their position in the hierarchy. This is borne out by our own discussions with managers in FE. There is undoubtedly a 'guardian' role, attempting to mitigate the potential impact of negative events by putting them into context for people or suggesting possible strategies as to how they might be addressed (Jameson, 2006). There is an obvious link here to telling a compelling story. One principal we spoke to was fond of writing to their staff, alongside information being circulated about the latest policy initiative. They would concentrate on making the potential consequences of any change meaningful for their college, and, importantly, suggest how they might respond positively to the challenge.

But the best leaders never let this 'guardian angel' role shield their people entirely from reality. We have referred in an earlier chapter to leaders having to *confront the brutal facts* (Collins, 2001). This ability to face up to reality but not lose hope is a crucial building block in what Collins calls *Level Five Leadership*, the highest level in a hierarchy of leadership effectiveness. Comforting followers with false hope is at best a short-term solution to hardship, and at worst a hugely demotivating strategy that destroys trust and undermines leadership credibility. An equally important leadership role, rather like Scrooge's final ghostly visitor in *A Christmas Carol* is that of helping people understand the potential consequences of a course of action and the less palatable aspects of what the future might bring. The kind of performance data we spoke of as necessary to making things happen in Chapter 7 will sometimes, inevitably, contain large amounts of bad news. Is this necessarily something to avoid? If not, how do we reconcile this with acting as 'guardian'?

As with most aspects of leadership, there is a balance to be struck here. If, as leaders, we want to develop leadership in our people, at whatever level, then it seems obvious that we must expose them, when necessary, to the harsh realities of the need for change. How else will they develop the resilience and *adaptive capacity* to respond positively to such challenges themselves (Bennis and Thomas, 2002)? Far from wrapping people in cotton wool, great leaders treat people like the responsible adults they (usually) are and talk honestly of the difficulties to be addressed. Churchill promised the nation nothing but *blood, toil, tears and sweat* in the dark days of May 1940, but that did not stop him having an unwavering belief in the Allies' ability to prevail over Nazism.

The guardian angel aspect of the leader's role lies in not allowing people to become *overwhelmed* by the scale of the external threat or challenge. They must therefore allow the organisation and people within it to feel the *pinch of reality*, to the degree that they can tolerate (Heifetz and Laurie, 1997). Discomfort can be an entirely constructive impulse, despair is generally not.

What is it leaders do to keep things positive?

Perhaps the most obvious point to make is that good leaders, as individuals, have a resilience that allows them to remain determined in the face of difficult circumstances. This 'glass half-full' mentality, described by one senior manager in FE as 'Let's have a go and see what we can do with this issue', is prized by leaders and valued in those who work for them. If they are by nature optimistic, this probably helps, as do passion, high energy levels and a sense of humour, particularly about themselves. If some of these are not in their nature, then they must be practised at reframing circumstances in such a way as to focus on the learning opportunities and potential solutions. We have already talked about the tendency of effective leaders to put setbacks and challenges into context as part of their ability to make people's work meaningful. This is how they help others to interpret issues more positively. Such leaders not only help to mitigate the *toxic emotions* associated with people in organisations, particularly those undergoing transformation, but also act as effective *toxin handlers* themselves, because they are able to defuse the distress of others without becoming worn down themselves (Frost, 2003).

TASK

Costas, the Head of the School of Electronic Engineering, has wandered into the office of his colleague, Svetlana, Head of the School of Business. He has just found out that the Senior Management Team have decided to merge his School with Motor Vehicle Maintenance and Repair.

Svetlana	*Oh, hi there, Costas. Sorry, did we have a meeting?*
Costas	*The b*****ds! No, really, the absolute b*****ds!*
Svetlana	*Only I'm just in the middle of something at the moment . . . Maybe we could grab half an hour at three-ish?*
Costas	*Well, that's it. It's all gone to pot. I'm not standing for this lying down. How could they? After all that I said?*
Svetlana	*I guess maybe we should talk about this now, then. Could this have anything to do with the debate over whether to merge your mob and Motor Vehicle?*
Costas	*Too b****y right! As of the start of next academic year apparently we will all belong to the School of Engineering and Motor Vehicle Studies, for goodness sake. I've already told my team I think it's wrong-headed and short-sighted. I'm drafting a letter to the Chair of Governors.*

Svetlana	Right. What is it you're hoping to do?
Costas	What am I going to do? I'm going to give it to the pompous twerp straight. All the reasons why this won't work.
Svetlana	No, I mean what outcome are you aiming for?
Costas	I should have thought that was obvious. I want it to be clear, when it all comes crashing down around their ears, that I was right all along.
Svetlana	So you don't expect them to change their mind?
Costas	No, that's just it. They can't now. It's all been ratified at board and signed off, would you believe?
Svetlana	And were they aware of your arguments against the move?
Costas	Oh, I should hope so. I addressed the board meeting personally a couple of weeks ago, and the Principal asked me to draft up a paper for them. Some b****y use that was!
Svetlana	So let me see if I've got this straight. You've been given the opportunity to put your case, in detail, against the merger of the two schools. You've lost the argument, and a decision has been made. Now you want to put a bee up the corporation's backside, even though you know that you cannot change the decision?
Costas	Well, what do you expect me to do, just roll over and let them do what they like?
Svetlana	They've already done that, Costas. It's their decision to make, and they've made it. Let me ask you a question. What is there that you can influence?
Costas	Well, obviously nothing! I'm just a humble cog in the great big fascist corporate machine, aren't I?
Svetlana	(Losing patience) Listen to me, you pathetic, self-pitying worm. Exactly how much do you suppose this impression of a petulant five-year-old is going to impress the people who may shortly be having to make decisions about your future role? Have you stopped to think how your team are feeling at the moment? I'm sure your little 'pep talk' must have been very inspiring. They're probably flinging themselves off the Brunel Building right now!

Svetlana's coaching may have its limitations, but what point is she trying to make to Costas? What if you were in Costas's position? What would be a practical and worthwhile strategy from here on? What would an excellent leader do?

Explain your recommendations.

DISCUSSION

A part of this 'healthy' response to adversity is knowing when to 'let go'. Effective leaders, while comfortable with taking responsibility and grasping the initiative, also learn to recognise when circumstances have moved matters beyond their control. At this point, further resistance becomes wasteful and the organisation must be helped to engage positively with whatever change has become inevitable.

If this appears contradictory at first, it is probably not surprising. Because another characteristic of successful leaders, which enables them to stay positive while facing up to trying circumstances, is their ability to handle ambiguity. Decisions in organisations are rarely, if ever, a matter of right and wrong. They concern shades of opinion, tricky estimates of risk and the attempt to predict all sorts of things that remain stubbornly resistant to accurate forecast. Half of the information may be missing and the half you have may be inaccurate. Leaders have to confront tough trade-offs, and get their people used to confronting them too (Heifetz and Laurie, 1997). Resilience is not just about managing frustrations but having the emotional capacity to tolerate uncertainty too, and hold two or more contradictory notions in one's head at the same time.

This is how leaders in FE that we spoke to could argue passionately against some aspect of national policy or funding change, then recognise when it had become inevitable and switch almost seamlessly to focus on implementing it better than any other college in the country. What is more, they saw no difficulty in reconciling in their own mind the idea that something was at odds with their values, but they would do it anyway to the best of their ability.

CLOSE FOCUS

Before we leave Svetlana and Costas entirely, you might like to reflect on how you could improve on Svetlana's coaching technique! What questions would you have asked to try to help Costas shift his mindset?

Another way in which excellent leaders encourage more positive thinking is by avoiding passivity on the part of their staff, because giving people the complacent feeling of all being well will paralyse them every bit as surely as creating a sense of panic. So, leaders need to ensure that the work of adapting to circumstance is shared around. One way of doing this is not to have all the answers. Leaders can let people feel the discomfort of adverse events by asking tough questions rather than trying to pretend that they have all the solutions. That way people can become engaged and, just as importantly, used to focusing on solutions, not problems.

Finally, leaders encourage people to concentrate on the positive aspects of any challenge by openly recognising and celebrating success. When times are tough and it seems that bad news is outweighing the good, we all need to feel that we are making progress, however slowly. This is where the kind of short-term milestones that we mentioned in Chapter 7 can be really useful. Used as opportunities for joint celebrations of achievement, they can help enormously to bolster people's belief that their team or organisation can prevail over what may otherwise seem like overwhelming odds.

The 'dark side'

At its best, this tendency to stay positive is rooted in a firm belief in people's appreciation of honesty, and their natural urge to succeed and put up with short-term discomfort for the benefit of longer-term achievements. Without some foundation in such values, without the balance of some ethical code, this dual role of guardian angel and honest bearer of harsh truths becomes distorted.

The desire to present information positively at all costs can result in reckless risk-taking or 'creative accounting'. How many stories have we heard over recent years of senior mangers 'cooking the books' to present a rosy picture of the organisation to stakeholders? At a lower level this might translate as fiddling performance figures, or exaggerating the achievements of students to make it appear objectives have been met, perhaps to secure funding or simply one's own job.

Conversely, unprincipled leaders might choose to overplay the potential risks and challenges of future change, either because they are unable to regulate their own anxiety in front of their team, or because they foolishly think this will 'motivate' them, or perhaps because they deliberately want to frighten people into making changes that they would otherwise legitimately question. Exposing people to the realities of what the organisation faces is only a constructive approach if people trust the leader to be straight with them (see Chapter 2, Connecting with people). If not, then followers may perceive all sorts of unworthy agendas and resist any attempt to engage them in the tough task ahead.

Issues for the Lifelong Learning sector

One of the biggest challenges for leaders in the Lifelong Learning sector is helping people through a period of continuing seismic change, not all of which will be prompted by independent decisions of their own about their teams and organisations. Inevitably, as in the past, government policy will have an impact upon the balance of business focus and student focus. Leaders will be having to find ways of reconciling their own personal and professional values with national initiatives which will undoubtedly affect the economic and social role their educational institutions play. They will continue to mediate between government, the community and their staff, in seeking to keep all stakeholders on board. They will need to implement strategies that help their organisations to make the most of the opportunities such change provokes, while creating a workplace ethic which most of their people can buy into. They will probably have to help people inside and outside the organisation to change their mindsets as their jobs become ever more outcomes-orientated. It goes without saying that handling ambiguity and keeping themselves and their teams focused on the positive will be a critical part of their role.

Self-evaluation and development

Are you by nature a cup half-full or a cup half-empty kind of person? Are you inclined to see all the possible problems with a strategy or plan of action, or do you get so excited about the idea that you fail to see how anything can go wrong, until it does? In Winnie the Pooh terms, are you a Tigger or an Eeyore? In reality we are not all natural optimists. Personality questionnaires will help you find out more about your profile, but the truth is you probably know this about yourself already. Just speak to family and friends.

If you are a positive personality to start with, much of what we have talked about will come more easily to you. But remember pessimists are useful too. Every team needs someone who will stay grounded and soberly assess risk while others are getting carried away. As a leader, however, you may need to find ways of preventing your natural pessimism or scepticism from making you appear negative. You may have to work harder at reframing issues in ways which allow you to see the opportunities and upside. One way of doing this is to ensure you talk these issues through with someone else on the team who may take a more optimistic perspective. Another is to talk things through with a coach or mentor. Reframing events for yourself will help you do it for others.

If you are good at seeing all the reasons why something cannot be done, try keeping this immediate response to yourself until you have deliberately translated every one of these objections into a possible solution. That way you can make the most of your critical sense without it becoming a drag on more positive members of the team. Alternatively, express your misgivings by asking the team searching questions, forcing them to challenge you back or suggest solutions. This is a much gentler and more empowering way of stress testing ideas than just raising objection after objection or listing all the reasons why nothing can be done.

How about your ability to handle ambiguity? Are you temperamentally the sort of person that likes to see issues in terms of right and wrong, of having correct or incorrect answers? Sometimes this depends on the kind of discipline we are from and whether we are used to problems that lend themselves to clear single answers. If this is something you want to develop further, then try leading a cross-departmental project, where lots of opinions and interests are involved. Ideally, try leading a people-related project, where the chances of a 'right' answer are slim. This kind of experience might help build your *adaptive* capacity and your ability to hold onto seemingly contradictory perspectives simultaneously.

Another idea is to look at developing your mentoring/coaching skills, so that you can help others to respond positively to uncertainty, without losing sight of the organisation's long-term vision and purpose. You can also help them to question long-standing beliefs and preconceptions that may be preventing them from adapting successfully to a changing organisational landscape (Gravells, 2006).

Finally, if you tend to be risk averse, you might encourage yourself and others to experiment more, taking action and trying new solutions when your heart tells you it feels right, rather than waiting for your head to be 100 per cent satisfied. Try getting more in touch with your intuition. If the results are not disastrous and you find you are learning from them, you may feel more confident of your ability to prevail in future!

Summary of key points

- Effective leaders tend to believe that we make our own luck and therefore find ways of responding positively to hardship and challenge.
- They understand the influence of the leader's mood on the motivation of the team.
- They expose people to enough of the 'harsh realities' of the team or organisation's position, while maintaining the conviction that a positive outcome is achievable.
- They enable people to develop this resilience themselves by asking tough questions, putting threats and challenges in context, helping them reinterpret issues, and encouraging action in the face of ambiguity and uncertainty.

In conclusion

In the preceding chapters we have explored seven key themes of leadership in the Lifelong Learning sector. We now go on, in the final two chapters, to provide you with an opportunity to apply this theoretical framework, in a flexible and integrated way, to some 'real-life' scenarios.

But first, Figure 8.1 (see page 104) helps summarise what we have covered in the previous seven chapters and provides some signposts to help you navigate your way through the scenarios that follow.

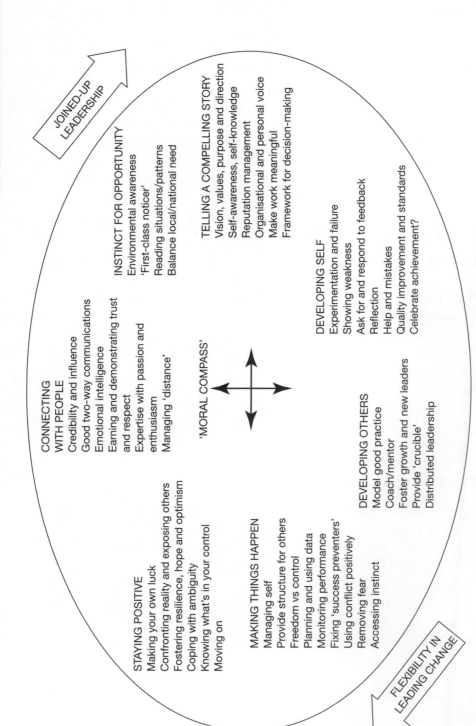

Figure 8.1 Leadership framework

9. Flexibility in leading change

CHAPTER OBJECTIVES

This chapter is designed to help you to:

- examine the context in which leaders in FE must engage with change;
- consider ways in which external change agents shape the range of operation of the FE team leader at all levels within the organisation;
- evaluate the ideas and theories covered in previous chapters as they apply to the leadership of change;
- examine the concept of 'change fatigue', its implications for the team leader and ways in which the problems it raises might be addressed;
- explore some models of change and apply them to the analysis of your own organisation and your leadership role within it;
- reflect upon and evaluate your own strengths and weaknesses as a leader in times of change.

Introduction

In some ways the title of this chapter is a misleading one. Although you will frequently find yourself leading your team *through* change, it is seldom that you yourself will be the originator or instigator of that change. In FE today it is generally recognised that change – to the curriculum, to funding, to the purpose of the organisation – is more often imposed externally through national and local policy decisions, or through necessities arising from the impact of these, than it is generated internally from within the institution itself. This pattern of what has been described by some FE leaders as *continual intervention* and *micro-management* by politicians (Nash, 2006, p5) has, many claim, resulted in *change fatigue* (ibid.). This, of course, has a number of profound implications for leadership at all levels.

Change fatigue

Whoever coined the term *change fatigue* probably had in mind that older expression 'battle fatigue' – an inability to function effectively, brought on by prolonged and unrelieved exposure to the high levels of stress encountered in combat. Coping with constant, relentless change over which we have little control can eventually have a similar, debilitating effect, particularly if we are to be held responsible for the ultimate success or failure of its implementation. The statistics are not encouraging. Up to 70 per cent of change initiatives are reckoned to fail (Higgs and Rowland, 2005). When we asked our focus group of middle managers and leaders to identify what they saw as the main barriers to their own effectiveness, an issue raised by all of them was the high level of stress generated by lack of control over change.

They are not unique in this, of course. Middle ranking leaders in most large organisations would probably make the same claim. It is claimed by some that much of the stress we associate with change stems from our unrealistic desire to control and predict the outcome (Firth, 1999). But where the FE college does differ from many other organisations is in the fact that even the senior 'executive' leadership must take its lead from the decisions made by external change agents. This is about more than that current buzz word 'responsiveness'. It is about having corporate goals, targets and even the values fundamental to the organisation set by outsiders. It is largely this lack of control over the rate and direction of change that generates 'change fatigue'. For this reason we need to be cautious in taking theories about leadership and change derived from the wider world of business and commerce and applying them uncritically to situations within an FE context, without first exploring their degree of relevance and 'fit'.

The external agents for change will be familiar to anyone working within FE. They include most notably the Department for Education and Skills (DfES) which sets the agenda, the curriculum and the mission for FE (as, for example, in DfES, 2006), the Learning and Skills Council (LSC) which sets the targets and largely controls the funding, and Lifelong Learning UK (LLUK) which sets the national standards for teaching and supporting learning in the sector, as well as the occupational standards for leadership. Changes or developments in any of these key areas will ultimately be made independently of the sector on which they will have an impact, 'consultations' not withstanding.

Many of the accepted models of change cope reasonably well with individual change initiatives. They are less helpful when applied to multiple, maybe conflicting, change processes all running concurrently, particularly if these are at least partly imposed. Given that it is impossible for everyone in an organisation to be comfortable with any particular change (Lumby and Tomlinson, 2000), motivating staff in the face of this constant change is a key challenge for leaders in Lifelong Learning (Withers, 2000). Externally imposed changes to the curriculum, to the balance of provision, to the funding formulae and to the purpose or mission of the sector all affect the task of leaders at every level within the organisation, from the head of section working against the clock to get revised programme specifications into place, to the head of school adapting their marketing strategy in the light of revised funding regulations, to the senior management team reworking the college's mission statement in the light of new legislation. All of these leaders may be concerned that they and their teams are showing signs of 'change fatigue'. But, aside from overhearing muttered comments of Oh no. Here we go again, what evidence might they find that this was so?

....

Task

Think for a moment about the implications of change fatigue in terms of the obstacles it presents to effective performance. How might it manifest itself in you and in members of your team? What challenges does it present to the team leader? You might like to jot down a list and compare it with ours in the discussion that follows.

....

Discussion

You will probably have identified some of the following as possible consequences of working in a climate of rapid and repeated change:

- decision-making becomes reactive rather than proactive;
- loss of control leads to loss of morale and/or confidence;
- the lack of periods of stability can mean there's no time to consolidate achievements or to regroup and review;
- forward planning becomes difficult because the ground rules may change;
- there is a lack of clarity about one's purpose or role;
- there is a loss of job satisfaction as a result of any of the above.

These in turn can manifest themselves in observable behaviours which you as team leader may find yourself having to address. Here, in effect, you encounter a fundamental dilemma of leadership, *because the one thing you can't do*, in these circumstances, is to remove the cause. *You can't slow down or interrupt the rate of change.* Some of these possible knock-on effects are indicated in Table 9.1. You may be able to add more from your own experience.

Change is clearly more than simply a rational, linear process. Because it frequently entails fundamental shifts in human behaviour and challenges to people's deeply-held beliefs about their role and sort of organisation they work in, change is inevitably an emotional journey and a complex process. The bald statistics tell us that not everything turns out as planned, and we have acknowledged already the extent to which much of the change we have to cope with is outside of our control. We cannot assume that merely by following a logical five-step process (or six or seven or whatever), we will suddenly find ourselves in complete control. Approaches to change based on assumptions of linearity are far more likely to fail, as are initiatives rooted in the notion that we, as leaders, will 'change' people's behaviour (Higgs and Rowland, 2005). The idea of a remote control device tuned in to one's team may be an attractive one but sadly fanciful. Individuals decide whether they are going to change, and even whether that will be an enthusiastic adjustment or a grudging one. Multiply this process by, say, 2,000 staff in an FE college

Table 9.1 Consequences of change fatigue

CONSEQUENCE OF CHANGE FATIGUE	OBSERVABLE BEHAVIOURS/INDICATORS
Reactive rather than proactive decision-making	Reluctance to come up with new ideas or take responsibility for innovation.
Loss of morale/confidence	Over-dependence on you, as leader. Lack of initiative. Poor performance.
No stability in which to consolidate and review	'Butterfly syndrome': always moving on to the next project. Failure to monitor and review new developments. Lots of good ideas, but little follow through.
Difficulty in long-term planning	'Short-termism'; failure to think things through. Loss of the 'big picture'. Each task/development seen in isolation. No joined-up thinking.
Individuals lacking clarity about their purpose or role	Lack of commitment. Tasks left undone. Tasks duplicated. Loss of motivation. Lack of enthusiasm. Loss of team spirit.
Loss of job satisfaction	Talented team members leaving. Grumbling. Loss of good will. Loss of team spirit.

and you can see why successful change is a complex business. As leaders, therefore, our role is surely to adapt successfully to change ourselves and help our people do likewise. But we cannot rely on providing certainty and answers to help our teams through such constant change. Indeed, as we pointed out in Chapter 8, we may even have to deliberately expose our people to the negative consequences of not changing. So what do we do?

Well, programmatic, linear approaches to change tend to emanate from the comfortable idea of an 'it' out there which needs to be changed (organisational structure, culture, processes, etc.). In truth organisations are generally mirrors of their leaders, and so the first thing that may need to change is you (Anderson, undated). How do you respond to change?

TASK

Go back to Table 9.1 earlier and, assuming that you can't *remove* the original cause of the behaviours, imagine there's a third column in this table in which you can jot down ways in which you could address these change fatigue indicators. You may find it useful to refer to your notes from previous chapters to ensure that you have considered as wide a range of responses and strategies as possible.

DISCUSSION

Table 9.2 lists some of the possible strategies you may have identified. We have cross-referenced them to the appropriate chapters in this book so that you can, if you wish, refresh your memory about how each or any of them can be applied in practice.

Table 9.2 Responses to the consequences of change fatigue

CONSEQUENCE OF CHANGE FATIGUE	INDICATOR	STRATEGY/RESPONSE
Reactive decision-making	Reluctance to come up with new ideas or take responsibility for innovation. Loss of the 'big picture'.	Model good practice. Emphasise purpose and direction. *Key chapters: 5 and 6.*
Loss of morale/confidence	Over-dependence on you, as leader. Lack of initiative. Poor performance.	Find things to praise. Foster growth. Provide coaching/mentoring. *Key chapters: 2 and 5.*
Lack of stability'	'Butterfly syndrome': always moving on to the next project. Failure to monitor and review new developments. Lots of good ideas, but little follow through.	Engage team in quality assurance procedures. Take action to establish monitoring and review. Model persistence. *Key chapters: 5, 6, 8.*
Difficulty in long-term planning	'Short-termism'; failure to think things through. Each task/development seen in isolation. No joined-up thinking.	Communicate vision, values, purpose and direction. Share information. Involve team in decision-making (e.g. through consultation) *Key chapters: 2, 4, 7.*
Lack of clarity about role/purpose	Lack of commitment. Tasks left undone. Tasks duplicated. Loss of motivation. Lack of enthusiasm. Loss of team spirit	Instil a sense of meaning. Tackle unacceptable performance. Place emphasis on team-building as well as task. *Key chapters: 2, 4, 6, 7.*
Loss of job satisfaction	Talented team members leaving. Grumbling. Loss of good will. Loss of team spirit.	Build confidence in the future. Celebrate achievement. Provide a crucible for growth. Generate trust. *Key chapters: 2, 5, 6.*

Successful change depends much more on the behaviour of leaders than most managers realise (Kelman, 2000). The way you, as leader, respond to the imperatives of change will have an enormous impact on the attitude of the team you lead. If you grumble, it's more likely that they'll grumble. If you demonstrate a high level of stress by running around like Basil Fawlty or by snapping and snarling at everyone who crosses your path, your team is likely to take this as a cue that a negative, counter productive response to change is perfectly OK. Of course, there's a fine line to be drawn here. We've placed an emphasis in previous chapters on the importance of authenticity in a leader. And indeed it's perfectly possible to acknowledge the stressfulness or frustrating nature of a situation while at the same time modelling a positive and professional attitude towards getting the job done. A great deal of this comes back to the issues and behaviours we explored in the previous chapter. Leading in the face of constant change is certainly one of the greatest tests of staying positive.

Leading the team safely through change

Let's have a look now at how some of this might work in practice. We're going to take a typically complicated 'real-life' situation; one where an initial, policy-induced change leads to others and the knock-on effects begin to present a real challenge to our leadership capacity to contain them and turn them in a positive direction. Another reason why change is so complex is that, not only are multiple changes happening in parallel, but they are all interconnected. Fixed goals become constraining as other people's actions affect our own objectives. Sometimes these connections are hard to predict resulting in unexpected outcomes. Our sense of security cannot be based entirely upon sound planning and implementation, but also upon a willingness and ability to adapt. We must be ready to sense connections in changing circumstances, to apply short-term tactical flexibility as well as long-term vision and strategy (Gravells, 2006). Rather than top-down change, this is back to the *adaptive leadership* we have mentioned before. (Heifetz and Laurie, 1997). Read through the scenario that follows. This is an opportunity to think how you might apply the various themes in our leadership framework in different combinations to different aspects and stages of the change process. It will be helpful if we keep in mind the multiple responsibilities of leaders at all levels in the face of change. These can be summarised in their simplest form as the responsibility to ensure that:

- the required change is successfully implemented;
- your team perform to the necessary standard;
- levels of motivation and commitment within the team are maintained.

Balancing these three imperatives is one of the key functions of leadership and is not dependent on any one style or approach. One of the things the following task will help you, as a leader, to do is to identify your own approach to achieving this balance.

TASK

Read carefully through the scenario which follows. We are going to ask you to (a) identify the issues and (b) decide how you will address them from the point of view of one of the leaders caught up in this situation.

All change!

Four years ago, Winterhill College, a general FE college serving a large market town and its surrounding rural area, was involved in a merger with the local sixth-form college. Although termed a 'merger', this was, in fact, more of a takeover, with the sixth form college becoming part of Winterhill College's Faculty of Adult and General Education. In the light of the Foster Report (2005) and the FE White Paper (DfES, 2006), the senior team and board of governors of Winterhill College have revised its vision statement to place added emphasis on the College's role as a skills provider. The words 'education' and 'development of individuals' have been cut and replaced by 'training' and 'serving the workforce'. Staff originally from the sixth-form college are finding this redefinition of their role and mission particularly difficult to accept. In addition, as a response to the funding changes, Adult Education provision has been cut drastically, as has most of the non-vocational provision. This, of course, is having a huge impact on the Faculty of Adult and General Education, which is now to lose its name and separate identity. Most of its remaining provision will be moved to the Faculty of Business and Computing, which will become known as the Faculty of Business and Communication. The teacher education provision will be moved centrally and managed by the Staff Development section of Human Resources.

For most staff in the faculty of Adult and General Education, this will be the second 'merger' in four years, and many also feel that their professional identity is being undermined. They know that redundancies are inevitable, and have been told that everyone in the Faculty, including its Head, will have to reapply for the jobs that will remain after the reorganisation goes ahead. Staff in the School of Computing are also feeling unhappy about this development, although their school and jobs will not be affected. The way they see it, the removal of the word 'Computing' from the Faculty title is an undermining of their status and an undervaluing of the work they do.

In exploring the issues and identifying your leadership strategies you may choose to address this from the point of view of:

- Head of the Faculty of Adult and General Education (FAGE);
- Head of the current Faculty of Business and Computing (FBC);
- Head of School for Computing;
- Head of School of Adult Education;
- all of them in turn, or as many of them as you would find useful!

We have included an organisation chart in the Appendix to help you establish your bearings. You will probably find it useful to make some notes as you think about your response, so that you can compare your ideas to those we set out below. You may also find it useful, in weighing the situation and choosing your strategy, to re-read the notes you made on Chapters 4, 7 and 8 of this book.

DISCUSSION

1. The issues

This is a painful and stressful situation for everyone concerned. Something like this will have touched the lives of almost everyone currently working in the sector, even if only indirectly. The obvious big issue here is about helping people to cope with change. This is radical change, too. For some it will mean the loss of their jobs; for others a loss of meaning and identity. There will also inevitably be a period of uncertainty during which staff in the FAGE will not know whether or not they will retain their jobs. No doubt there will be anger, too, and resentment. And, of course, that most basic of emotions which change can often trigger: fear. If we set these out as a list:

stress; loss; uncertainty; anger; resentment; fear

it begins to look more like a job for a counsellor, a doctor or a social worker than for some poor rushed-off-their-feet team leader in FE, particularly when that team leader is probably feeling all those same emotions themselves. These are what we might call the 'people issues'. To address them we will need to call upon all those qualities and skills which we explored in Chapter 2 – qualities and skills which enable us to connect with people.

But there is also another set of issues. These are about organisational effectiveness and survival, and about responsiveness to the sector's mission as defined by external forces. One of the things we see in this scenario – and one of problems that make it so difficult from a leadership point of view – is an apparent collision between the needs of the organisation and the needs of the individuals who work there. One task for all the leaders involved here will be to address this, to resolve it where they can and to ameliorate the effects where no resolution is possible.

2. What can the Heads of Faculty do?

There is a danger in a situation such as this that there will be role polarisation. In other words, the two faculty heads may be seen in terms of 'hero' and 'villain' by those who feel they have most to lose from the changes. In this case the Head of FBC may well be viewed as the villain, extending her territorial claim to annexe the most viable courses in the other faculty. The Head of FAGE, correspondingly, may be viewed as the underdog, another hapless victim of change. Or – and perhaps this is worse – an underdog whose failure to protect his team has left them exposed to anxiety and loss and all those other negative feelings we've listed above. This sort of polarisation, 'this versus that', the framing of the world in terms of opposites, is something the human mind is very good at. We just seem to have a tendency to think that way. And the situation we're currently considering unfortunately provides ample opportunity to apply just that sort of knee-jerk interpretation. The Heads of Faculty may be seen as:

Good	versus	Bad
Weak	versus	Strong
Loser	versus	Winner
Caring	versus	Uncaring
Compassionate	versus	Personally ambitious

and so on. Now, there are a number of dangers here. If you find yourself labelled the 'good guy' in this sort of situation it is very, very tempting to graciously accept the role, lead your troops to the high morale ground and denounce the organisation as 'uncaring' or whatever other criticisms you may care to throw at it. This, however, would not be leadership. This would be a personal crusade or even an ego trip. And, if you find the finger pointing at you instead as 'bad guy', you'll find it very difficult to gain the trust and co-operation you'll need to lead effectively through this change. In other words, if leaders allow this polarisation to happen, they will all find themselves in a no-win situation. A key consideration for leaders at all levels, therefore, is to pre-empt or challenge this kind of polarised thinking before it can get a hold. This means, if possible, presenting a united front with other colleagues in leadership roles, and acknowledging the 'people issues' while at the same time emphasising the purpose and direction of the organisation, the factors which have necessitated this change. In other words, such a situation will require you to tell a compelling story (Chapter 6) which gives meaning to what is happening, both in terms of individuals' consequent experiences of uncertainty and of the shared vision and values of the organisation as a whole. No pressure there, then.

The Head of the Faculty of Adult and General Education (FAGE) is at risk here of being cast in the role of 'good guy' or 'underdog'. Either of these labels will undermine his leadership effectiveness. His best course, therefore, will be to align himself firmly with the forces of change, draw on his skills at connecting with people and provide a model of staying positive. He will need to ensure that the processes of change remain as transparent as possible so that his team is not left to guess or speculate unnecessarily about what might be happening. And he will need to be seen to be working in a professional and collegiate manner with the Head of FBC, and all others involved, towards a shared, organisational goal. This is a tall order, and one demanding the highest levels of professionalism.

The Head of the current Faculty of Business and Computing (FBC) will need to take exactly the same approach. She, however, may find herself somewhat hampered by being labelled the 'bad guy' in all this, both by those whose jobs are at risk in FAGE and by staff in the School of Computing, who take the change of name as an indication that they are undervalued. As we're all aware, it's much harder to shrug off the label of villain once you've been cast in that role. The head of FBC, therefore, will need to work very hard at winning hearts and minds, at building and sustaining positive relationships as the proposed changes are implemented, and at listening and communicating. This is a pretty tall order, too.

3. What can the Heads of School do?

In this situation the Heads of School have two main roles:

- as team leader they must look after the needs of their team;
- as part of the organisational leadership structure they must work to effectively implement the change.

Again, we can see potential for role conflict here, as these two imperatives will, at times, appear to be mutually exclusive. This again is the tension between the organisational and the personal voice which we explored in Chapter 6. But the Heads of School are more likely to avoid being hampered by 'good guy/bad guy' labels. This means it should be more straightforward for them to give an effective lead to their teams by modelling a professional approach while at the same time acknowledging and responding to the people issues – particularly the fears and anxieties – that this change inevitably engenders.

To summarise, then, the skills and strategies required to lead a team through a situation of this kind will include:

- providing a model of professionalism;
- listening;
- keeping communication open and maintain a high level of transparency;
- maintaining a balance between organisational and personal voice;
- pre-empting or challenging polarised thinking ('good guy/bad guy');
- giving a lead by staying positive;
- aligning firmly with the forces of change;
- being seen to be working in a professional and collegiate manner with others involved;
- telling a compelling story which makes sense of individuals' experiences as well as of the shared vision and values of the organisation as a whole;
- working constantly at winning hearts and minds.

CLOSE FOCUS

In the task you've just completed, we asked you to consider the strategies open to leaders at two different levels within the organisation: Heads of Faculty and Heads of School. In our discussion, however, very little difference has emerged between these two levels. Does this ring true in your own experience? Do you think there would be differences in the skills and strategies required at different levels of leadership in a situation such as this? And if so, how would you identify these differences?

DISCUSSION

We can try to illustrate in Figure 9.1 how the various skills and strategies that we have talked about in this book might be applied in a flexible way to help people through complex change.

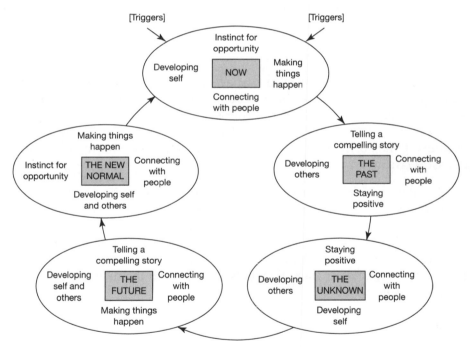

Figure 9.1 Framework for change
(Adapted from Wallace and Gravells, 2006)

This framework for change incorporates ideas from a number of eminent thinkers on the topic, including William Bridges, Peter Senge, Edgar Schein, John Kotter and Richard Barrett, to name but a few.

'Now'

Change is usually the result of some combination of internal and/or external triggers. In the case of Winterhill College, the Foster Report (2005) and subsequent White Paper (DfES, 2006) combined with funding cuts in Adult Education provision has led to FAGE losing its separate identity. Whatever the trigger, successful change generally starts with an understanding of where we are now and why.

This means being sensitive to the environment, listening to different accounts in order to appreciate where different interest groups may be coming from, and what the strengths and opportunities might be, not just the problems (*Instinct for opportunity*). But it may also mean examining hard financial and performance data in order to assess what options are available (*Making things happen*). Before rushing in to change anything, the managers at Winterhill College must be sure that they have had a genuine dialogue with staff, understand the reasoning behind the existing structure and how different groups of staff view the current challenge (*Connecting with people*). They may want to seek feedback and reflect on perceived mistakes in the past in order to continuously improve how the college responds to such challenges (*Developing self*).

'The past'

One of the most common mistakes managers make when faced with change is to 'trash the past'. Enthusiastic 'new brooms' come into a department and criticise all that has gone before, regardless of merit, in order to justify their own appointment. Staff in the FAGE will already be feeling superfluous. Recognising the positive contribution all teams have made to the college in the past is crucial.

If the Winterhill College managers are shrewd they will build a vision of what is over and what is not, and communicate this clearly to staff (*Telling a compelling story*) while at the same time showing respect for what has been achieved in the past (*Connecting with people*). They will be unambiguous about who and what must change (*Staying positive*), but support people and help them to adjust their 'mental models' to cope with the new reality (*Developing others*).

'The unknown'

Change takes time. In spite of a clear picture of where we want to end up, we frequently end up somewhere else, and in the meantime we may have to cope with weeks or months of not knowing where we are or whether we will get anywhere at all.

Managers at Winterhill College will need to handle this uncertainty themselves and work hard to focus on a positive outcome (*Staying positive*). They might help people to cope with it by encouraging experimentation and new ideas, accepting occasional failure as helpful learning (*Developing others*).

They might also use short-term action planning and review, so that people can see progress, however slight, and feel confident that change is happening (*Making things happen*). Most of all, they should be highly visible, available to listen to people's concerns, ensuring that no one feels isolated or ignored (*Connecting with people*).

'The future'

Let us assume that the structural changes at Winterhill College have now been achieved. Roles have changed and those whose jobs were lost have gone. The combined faculty is now in place and looks something like what was originally planned. As the future takes shape, the managers make a point of reminding people of that vision, the purpose behind the changes and what they were designed to achieve (*Telling a compelling story*).

They also review performance measures in order to celebrate early successes and try to prioritise actions, which will bring about 'quick wins' (*Making things happen*). But in helping people adjust to this new future, they do not just focus on processes and structures. They engage people in developing the culture and values of the new faculty, appealing to hearts as well as minds by painting a compelling picture of all it will achieve (*Connecting with people*). They use mentoring and coaching to help people adjust and develop in their new roles, including themselves (*Developing self and others*).

'The new normal'

Anyone who has made a New Year's resolution understands the fragility of change and how good intentions slip back into old behaviours so easily when the pressure is on. Working in a new way once or twice does not guarantee permanent change.

For Winterhill College to really embed the changes in its new department, it must continue to monitor performance and reinforce new ways of working, adjusting things where necessary to integrate the new structure. (*Making things happen*). Leaders will need to recognise the difference between grudging compliance and genuine behaviour change, which stems from new learning and a shift in underlying assumptions (*Developing self and others*). They will need to read what is going on around them well in order to reinforce progress and ensure that knock-on effects to other departments are managed (*Instinct for opportunity*).

But change will only truly be embedded when people do not just do things differently but feel and think differently too. Understanding the emotional journey for each individual and responding to this constructively requires a good deal of emotional intelligence (*Connecting with people*). Effective leaders recognise what they can and cannot control, and realise that lasting change must be accepted and not imposed.

Summary of key points

In this chapter we have:

- considered the impact of external change agents on leadership issues in FE;
- applied the ideas and theories covered in previous chapters to the leadership of change;
- explored the concept of 'change Sfatigue';
- examined some models of change;
- provided opportunities for you to evaluate your own strengths and weaknesses as a leader in times of change.

10. Joined-up leadership

CHAPTER OBJECTIVES

This chapter is designed to help you to:

- examine the concept of 'joined up leadership' and analyse its advantages;

- consider ways in which a 'joined-up' approach to leadership can be applied at different levels of leadership in a range of work situations;

- evaluate the ideas and theories covered in previous chapters and apply them to a variety of leadership challenges;

- recognise the need for balance between taking a holistic, joined-up approach to leadership and being aware of your own leadership strengths and weaknesses.

Introduction

In the middle section of this book we defined and explored a number of qualities and skills which are central to our definition of effective leadership. They include: connecting with people; developing an instinct for opportunity; developing yourself and your team; telling a compelling story; taking action; and remaining positive in the face of setbacks. In the previous chapter we tried to show how leaders reflect these themes in dealing specifically with change. In this chapter we want to emphasise the importance to you, the team leader, at whatever level you're operating within the organisation, of 'joined-up leadership'. This means being able to draw on any combination of these qualities and skills, according to the situation and circumstance. In this chapter we'll be looking at some scenarios which require you to do just that, and asking you to think your way through them, applying what you have learnt about these facets of leadership in order to suggest ways to address or resolve a range of leadership dilemmas.

As you work through the tasks which follow each scenario, you may find it useful to make some notes. This will allow you to compare your own reading of the situation with the analysis we present to you after each task, under the heading of Discussion. There may be some instances in which you disagree with our analysis of the situation. This is all to the good. In the real world of FE and Lifelong Learning it is frequently the case that there are no 'right' answers; and certainly, as this book stresses, there is always room for a range of leadership styles and approaches. Indeed, sometimes it is only possible to be definite about what would be categorically the wrong thing to do! And so if you are using this text to support part of a formal programme in professional development you will no doubt find it interesting to compare notes with others and discover how far their preferred approach is consistent with, or differs from, your own.

TASK

Read through the scenario below and then, bringing your leadership skills and knowledge to bear, address the tasks which follow. For contextual information you may wish to refer to the summary organisation chart in the Appendix.

Scenario 1

Rochelle is a Basic Skills lecturer who has been asked by her Head of School to step in as acting Section Leader while the current post-holder is on maternity leave. Although she has been teaching in the college longer than her three colleagues in the Basic Skills team (and perhaps this was the reason she was chosen to step in), she is the only one who still hasn't completed her Minimum Core Basic Skills teaching qualification. She has also needed regular help from other team members in planning her lessons and compiling her portfolio. The news of her new role has therefore come as something of a surprise to her colleagues, and none of them is very happy about it.

On her first day in her new role she announces that she's going to make some changes.

'What sort of changes?' asks Lee, cautiously.

'I don't know yet,' says Rochelle.

Later she bumps into another member of the team, Billie, who for the last year or so has been Rochelle's unofficial mentor, helping her develop ideas and resources.

'Guess what!' says Billie excitedly. 'I've managed to get a ticket for Wimbledon. Centre court!'

'You'll need to fill in a leave of absence form,' says Rochelle primly.

'Well yes, obviously. I was just . . .'

'And it needs to be done straight away.'

'I know. I know about leave of absence forms, Rochelle. I was just . . . '

'Well just make sure you do it,' says Rochelle, and walks away.

At the end of that day, Lee and Billie and their other colleague, Karl, are talking all this over in the car park. Lee is anxious, Billie is outraged and Karl – who feels his qualifications and experience make him the natural choice for acting Section Head – is threatening to resign.

'She can't even b****y teach!' he says.

'She can't even plan a lesson,' says Billie. 'She's even phoned me at home a couple of times on a Sunday morning, panicking and asking for advice.'

'The most worrying thing,' says Lee quietly, 'is that she doesn't even realise she's not up to it.'

No, we're not going to ask you to identify what Rochelle did wrong, because that would be too easy! What we'd like you to do is to do is this:

1. Identify and note down the key issues that the Head of School's decision raises in terms of its immediate impact on the section.

2. Now look at this scenario from a whole-school perspective. What are the leadership issues here?

3. The team's objections to this temporary promotion centre around Rochelle's difficulties with teaching. In your view, is this a relevant issue? And if so, why?

DISCUSSION

1. What are the key issues in terms of impact on the Section?

Your answer to this question probably includes some or all of the following:

- *The section will not be well led.* Even from this short scenario we can see that Rochelle is falling into some classic leadership errors. For example, she expresses her determination to make some changes, not because change is necessary (she's not even sure yet what she wants to change!), but presumably because she wants to 'make her mark'. She's failing to connect with members of her team or earn their respect – adopting instead a distant and officious approach. She isn't demonstrating self-knowledge, nor modelling good practice. We don't know what her predecessor was like. It's just conceivable that Rochelle may be an improvement – but it hardly seems likely.

- *This appointment will cause resentment among the team.* OK. Tough. Appointments sometimes do cause initial resentment. It often can't be helped. A measure of good leadership is whether such initial ill-feeling can be overcome and replaced with trust and a sense of teamwork. But in this case the situation is exacerbated by the fact that (a) the person appointed appears to be the section's weakest link, and (b) the appointee immediately goes on to demonstrate why her promotion was probably a very bad decision. Will she be able to recover the situation and win over the hearts and minds of her team? The way things are going, this seems unlikely.

- *This appointment will cause anxiety.* Again, that's often the way when a leader is newly appointed. What will they be like? What changes will they make? Will we get on with each other? But there is potential for more than the baseline anxieties in this scenario. The team has no faith in its leader. If anything is designed to induce anxiety at work, that certainly is. Moreover, the team may well now be feeling anxious about their position within the organisation as a whole. If such a disastrous decision could be made, what does that say about the value the college puts on their own ability and hard work? Or about communication within the organisation? Or about its priorities and values? And let's not forget Rochelle herself. She may be feeling more anxious than anyone (unless Lee is correct in the assumption that she lacks self-knowledge), and a leader with anxieties about her own role and abilities will find it doubly difficult to alleviate the anxieties of her team.

- *This appointment will cause loss of motivation.* Of course it will. From the team's point of view, in behaviourist terms, it seems that the least able, least qualified person has been rewarded with promotion while the hard work and ability of other team members has gone unrecognised. It wouldn't be surprising, therefore, if the rest of the team began asking themselves, 'Why bother?'

- *There is a risk that this appointment may have a negative impact on learners.* There are two ways in which this might happen. Lowered staff morale may lead to lowered standards of performance in the classroom, and/or the level of subject expertise of the new Section Leader may be insufficiently sound to facilitate or sustain the necessary quality of teaching and learning within the section.

- *There is a risk that an insecure leader will compensate with bullying behaviour.* We get a glimpse of this possibility in the exchange between Rochelle and Billie. A leader who feels insecure or unsure in their role may find it difficult to show or admit to any weakness. If they find themselves unable to generate trust or lead by example, their fall-back position may be officiousness or hectoring which can too easily degenerate into bullying. We've probably all – unfortunately – encountered a leader like this at some time. We can make something positive of this, however, by keeping them in mind as a dreadful example of what we should avoid at all costs. In the scenario we've just read, Rochelle's behaviour doesn't qualify as bullying, any more than the team's collective outrage does. But in a situation such as this everyone needs to be on their guard to ensure that matters don't escalate to a point where that line is crossed.

2. What are the whole-school leadership issues?

In your answer you've probably identified some or all of the following:

- *There has been a lack of transparency.* A decision has been made which affects an entire section, but the grounds for such a decision have not been made clear. The temporary promotion hasn't been opened up for applications from other members of the team. There appears to have been no formal application, interview or selection. No one knows what it is that has qualified the appointee for the role over and above any other team member. In other words, no one knows what's going on or why. Is there some wider plan they don't know about? Why were they left out of the loop? This is how trust is lost and conspiracy theories start.

- *What could be behind this apparently ill-judged decision?* It's possible to read a number of things into this decision which may reflect on the leadership of the school as a whole. For example:

- We could take it to imply that communication within the school is poor, or that at the very least the Head of School is failing to connect with, or listen to, what is going on at the chalk face. At the very least, the decision suggests a lack of knowledge about the team dynamic and the strengths and weaknesses within the team.

- An alternative interpretation would suggest that there was a lack of integrity or failure of the moral compass on the part of the Head of School, who may have made the decision based on the desire to temporarily appoint a 'puppet' Head of Section in order to personally exert more direct control over that section of the school.

- Or perhaps this appointment was an audacious but inspired risk, an attempt to create capability, based on the belief that she'll grow into the role. If so, this Head of School needs to remember that even decisions made with the best of intentions can have negative consequences and that their implementation still needs careful monitoring.

- *There's a need within this school for CPD or mentoring for newly appointed leaders at all levels,* including temporary, acting leaders. But we have to ask, who would do the mentoring here? Like us, you're probably having your doubts about the Head of School as a useful role model in this situation.

- *There appears to be a need within this school for joined-up thinking.* It appears from the scenario that one problem (the need for a temporary Section Leader) has been solved at the cost of creating several more – and very serious ones at that – including: losing the trust of the team; undermining their motivation; and posing a threat to the quality of teaching and learning. This is what can happen when a leader fails to take into account the wider picture.

3. In your view, are Rochelle's difficulties with teaching a relevant issue here? And if so, why?

Our answer to this has to be 'yes', and for a number of reasons. All of her team recognise that their newly appointed temporary leader has difficulties with her own classroom practice. Some of them have been in the position of having to provide her with continuing and substantial help in this area of professional expertise. As a consequence of this she will inevitably encounter difficulty in:

- winning the trust of the team on pedagogical and classroom issues;
- modelling good classroom practice for her team;
- earning the respect of her team as a fellow professional;
- providing continuing professional development for her team;
- rewriting her own poor reputation;
- demonstrating a willingness and ability to take on board feedback about her own professional performance.

Whole-college issues

In addressing this task you may also have found yourself touching on whole-college issues. It is a feature of joined-up leadership that you will tend to look not only at a specific issue but also at the whole picture – the context in which the issue has arisen. So, for example, you have perhaps found yourself drawing up a mental checklist of the questions you'd want to put to the senior management of this college, given half a chance. These might include questions about:

- whether the college implements a coherent leadership strategy;
- to what extent this includes future planning;
- how the Occupational Standards for Leadership and Management in FE are implemented and monitored;
- how appraisals operate and what use is made of the data gathered;
- how career progression and succession are managed within the college.

TASK

Now that you've had an opportunity to analyse the implications of Scenario 1, we're going to ask you to keep your leadership hat on and consider ways in which the situation might be addressed or even resolved. In framing your answers to the questions which follow we hope you will draw upon some of the key points we have covered in the previous chapters and think about how they might be applied in this situation. You might want to make a note of your ideas and then compare them to what we have to say in the discussion below.

Here are the questions we'd like you to consider:

1. What could be done to address this situation at a section level, by personnel within the section? How far is it recoverable? What advice would you give to Rochelle? What advice would you give to her colleagues?

2. Now imagine that you've suddenly stepped in as replacement Head of School and have been made aware of this situation. What would you do?

3. And if you found yourself in the role of Head of Faculty? What lessons would you draw from what's going on in the Basic Skills section? Would any action on your part be appropriate, and if so, what action?

DISCUSSION

1. What could be done to address this situation at a section level, by personnel within the section?

Your answer probably included some or all of the following:

● *How far is it recoverable?* There are very few situations which are not to some extent recoverable, so we can allow ourselves some guarded optimism about this one. In considering this question you will probably have found yourself thinking back to what we've said in previous chapters about: using conflict constructively (Chapter 7); facing struggles and moving on (Chapter 8); respect, recognition and relationships (Chapter 2); and creating capability (Chapter 6). It will certainly take skilful leadership and careful nurturing to help the section to regain its confidence and renew its bonds as a team. In our view, this would ideally be a role for the Head of School. But given that he or she has created this situation in the first place, we would probably look to the Head of Faculty to take the lead in jump-starting the section's recovery.

● *What advice would you give to Rochelle?* There are several steps Rochelle could take in order to improve the situation. In the short term she could concentrate on building up her relationship with colleagues rather than treating them officiously (Chapter 2). She could ask for and respond to feedback, and she could acknowledge her inexperience and weaknesses and ask for help (Chapters 4 and 5). In the longer term she could ask to be allocated a mentor in order to help her to develop her leadership skills (Chapter 8). If your advice to her was, 'Resign!' that's not only defeatist, it's cheating!

● *What advice would you give to her colleagues?* On the face of it, her team seem to be powerless in this situation, but they do have a very important choice here. They can choose to stop framing this as a story of unfairness with themselves as passive victims of an injustice or an error of judgement, and can choose instead to construe it as an opportunity to develop their teamwork and communication and to help their temporary leader to adapt positively to her new role. Adopting an outraged and resentful attitude is unlikely to result in anything but more negativity. So what does this mean in practical terms? Well, for a start they can model the professional behaviour expected of the team, including its leader, by maintaining all the usual social courtesies, including listening to what their team leader has to say and giving constructive feedback. The other thing they can do is to give her time to settle into the role before passing judgement. It may be that she proves to be every bit as disastrous a leader as they feared. If this is the case, they would be well advised that it's not part of the mutually supportive remit of a team to 'carry' a poor leader.

2. What would you do if you were to step in now to replace the existing Head of School?

Your answer probably included some or all of the following:

- Set up a mentor for Rochelle (yourself, perhaps?) to help her to develop the necessary skills and qualities for leadership of a small team.
- Consider the option of setting up a rotating team leadership during the period that the current post-holder is on maternity leave.
- Listen to the team, collectively and as individuals, and broker a fresh start.
- Take immediate action to challenge any unacceptable behaviour or failure to adequately carry out designated roles.

3. If you found yourself in the role of Head of Faculty, what lessons would you draw from what's going on in the Basic Skills section? Would any action on your part be appropriate, and if so, what action?

This is an interesting one. Your role at this level would be very much about giving a lead in terms of vision and values, and winning hearts and minds. If you're an effective Head of Faculty, your communication skills, willingness to listen and regular walkabouts will have made you aware of exactly what's going on and how everyone is feeling about it. As the scenario stands, it could be difficult for you to find a reason for any direct intervention at this stage. It is not inconceivable, however, that you could find yourself faced sooner or later with a delegation of disgruntled staff from this section, asking you to intervene on their behalf. This then becomes a very delicate situation between yourself and the Head of School, and you would probably want to go back and re-read Chapters 2 and 7 before deciding on a way forward!

TASK

Read through Scenario 2 below and then, bringing your leadership skills and knowledge to bear, address the tasks which follow. For contextual information you may find it useful to look again at the college's organisation chart in the Appendix.

Scenario 2

The Faculty of Business and Communication is having some difficulty in establishing the quality of its 14–16 provision. This may be partly because there is still resistance from staff to the idea of teaching younger learners. With the exception of the School of Computing, where staff find the younger learners to be keen and well motivated, there is a marked lack of enthusiasm among most of those who do teach on these programmes. This is particularly the case in the School of Business. A key objection from many of the staff in that School is that the younger learners create a disruptive atmosphere which is adversely affecting the motivation and attendance of mature groups of HNC and Foundation Degree students.

The Head of Faculty calls her Heads of School together to discuss the situation.

1. If you were Head of Faculty, what would be your desired outcomes from this meeting?

2. What are the most important skills or qualities that you'd need to draw on in this meeting to achieve the outcomes you desire?

DISCUSSION

1. Firstly then, what outcomes do you want from this meeting?

One way to look at this is to divide your desired outcomes into operational or 'hard' outcomes – for example, to arrive at agreed strategies for managing student behaviour and providing the necessary professional development to build staff confidence and motivation – and collateral or 'soft' outcomes – such as retaining the good will of all three Heads of School and reaching an agreement about the shared vision and purpose of the Faculty. The 'hard' outcomes are about *what* needs to be done, and the 'soft' outcomes will depend upon *how* you do it – whether you do it in a way that generates commitment, enthusiasm and a spirit of teamwork. You will only have partly succeeded in your purpose if you leave the meeting having 'agreed' a way forward but having in the process offended or alienated one or more of the Heads of School. In other words, we're looking here at arriving at that balance between sustaining productive relationships and achieving the task in hand which we explored in some detail in Chapter 2.

2. So, that being the case, what skills or qualities did you decide you would need in order to make this meeting a successful one?

We've already mentioned the relationship–task balance. You probably also identified some or all of the following:

- generating trust: winning hearts and minds;
- communicating clearly and sharing all relevant information;
- listening;
- recognising and respecting the views of others (though not necessarily acting on them);
- maintaining courtesy;
- emphasising teamwork;
- telling a compelling story: promoting the vision for the Faculty and selling the future it offers;
- asking for and responding to feedback;
- celebrating what has already been achieved;

- modelling good practice in terms of team leadership for your Heads of School to follow;
- instilling in them a sense of hope and optimism;
- and, of course, *taking action*.

This really *is* joined-up leadership. And this list of skills and strategies is a pretty useful one to take into any meeting!

TASK

Read through Scenario 3 below and then consider the questions which follow. We've met Sean and Tucker earlier, in Chapter 2. Their encounter there wasn't a very successful one. Let's see whether Sean has learnt anything from that and brushed up on his leadership skills.

Scenario 3

Sean is Tucker's Section Head. He is also acting as his mentor while Tucker completes his Level Three teaching qualification. This involves formally observing Tucker's teaching on six occasions and assessing him against the National Standards. He has so far observed Tucker four times, but each time the lesson has been a fiasco and Tucker has requested that the observation be treated as a 'trial run'. Following the fourth observation, Sean sits down with him in an empty classroom to give him some feedback.

Sean   *So how do you feel that lesson went?*

Tucker *Not good. I think we'd better take that one as another trial run, mate, don't you?*

Sean   *Thing is, Tucker, I don't think we can keep on doing that. It's getting to the point where we're not going to be able fit in six more observations before your assessments are due in.*

Tucker *Come on, mate! You're here all the time. I'm here all the time. What's the problem?*

Sean   *Well, one problem is, I've got other things to do.*

Tucker *Yeah? Well maybe you'd better sort me out a different mentor if you're too 'busy'.*

Sean   *And the other thing is a matter of principle, really. If I just keep on waiting for you to teach a decent lesson before I write it up, it's not really a reliable or valid assessment, is it?*

Tucker *What do you mean, 'Waiting for me to teach a decent lesson?'*

Sean   *Well, that's what you're asking me to do, isn't it?*

Tucker *So first of all you're telling me you haven't got time to do it. And then you're telling me I'm so crap you'd have to wait for ever to see me teach a decent lesson? Thanks a lot, mate.*

Sean	*That's not what I'm saying. But look, I'm going to assess you on this one I've just seen. So do you want to talk first about why you think it didn't go very well?*
Tucker	*It's those students, isn't it. They're rubbish. They don't listen. They can't sit still . . .*
Sean	*They're OK when I teach them.*
Tucker	*That's because they know they've got to behave with you. They know you're the Section Head. That's why they're OK for you.*
Sean	*Or could it also be because I give them interesting things to do and don't try to dictate notes to them for thirty minutes at a stretch?*
Tucker	*I don't like your tone, mate.*
Sean	*Well, I don't like you calling me 'mate', you awkward . . . Tucker.*

Oh dear. So no change there, then.

1. What seem to be the leadership issues emerging in this scenario? (You might find it useful to jot these down as a list.)

2. Can you identify any strengths here that Sean could build on?

3. If you were Sean's mentor and could ask him three questions to get him reflecting about his performance here, what questions would you ask?

DISCUSSION

1. Leadership issues

One of the key issues here, which you probably identified the last time we met these two characters, concerns the lack of clarity about the parameters of their relationship. Sean is Tucker's team leader and line manager. But he is also his mentor. And – in Tucker's view at least – his 'mate'. The resulting role conflict makes their professional interaction difficult for both of them. We can see Sean jumping between roles here:

Friend	*'They're OK when I teach them.'*
Mentor	*'So how do you feel that lesson went?'*
Team Leader/ Head of Section	*'Look, I'm going to assess you on this one I've just seen.'*

It's likely that most of the leadership issues you've listed arise directly or indirectly from this lack of clarity. Ours certainly do. Have a look and see how your list compares to the following:

- achieving the right balance between formality and friendliness;
- being courteous, even when exasperated;

- modelling professional behaviour, even under provocation;
- finding an acceptable way to address unacceptable behaviour;
- handling difficult situations without making it a personal issue;
- keeping parameters clearly drawn while still remaining approachable.

CLOSE FOCUS

All of the behaviours listed above are balancing acts which are necessary at every level of leadership. It could be argued, however, that such a balancing act is most difficult in the front line of the organisation, at section level, where the hierarchy is quite flat and the difference in status between section leader and members of their team is less apparent than the difference in their levels of responsibility would suggest.

1. Would you agree with this argument?

2. What evidence would you present to support your case?

3. If there are aspects of this balancing act which you believe get easier at more senior levels, which ones are they, and why?

---

2. Sean's strengths

He does demonstrate some potential strengths here which could be developed. They include:

- being decisive and taking action: I'm going to assess you on this one;
- being honest: Well, one problem is, I've got other things to do;
- getting to the point and not beating about the bush: If I just keep on waiting for you to teach a decent lesson before I write it up, it's not really a reliable or valid assessment, is it?

3. Three questions to encourage reflection

The three questions we'd put to Sean are:

- What are some of the ways you can establish your leadership when the status 'gap' between yourself and your team is very narrow?
- What are the difficulties and the advantages that arise from acting as mentor to someone for whom you are also team leader/line manager?
- What is the point at which your conversation with Tucker (above) first took a wrong turn, and how would you handle that interchange differently if you could go back and do it again?

Summary of key points

In this chapter we have:

- examined the concept of 'joined-up leadership' in the context of some practical scenarios;
- analysed the practical advantages of this approach;
- looked at ways in which a 'joined-up' approach to leadership can be applied at different levels in the organisation;
- applied the ideas and theories covered in previous chapters to a variety of practical leadership challenges;
- argued the need for balance between taking a holistic approach and being aware of your own leadership strengths and weaknesses.

Partial organisation chart of Winterhill College, showing the relationship between characters, faculties and schools which appear in this book.

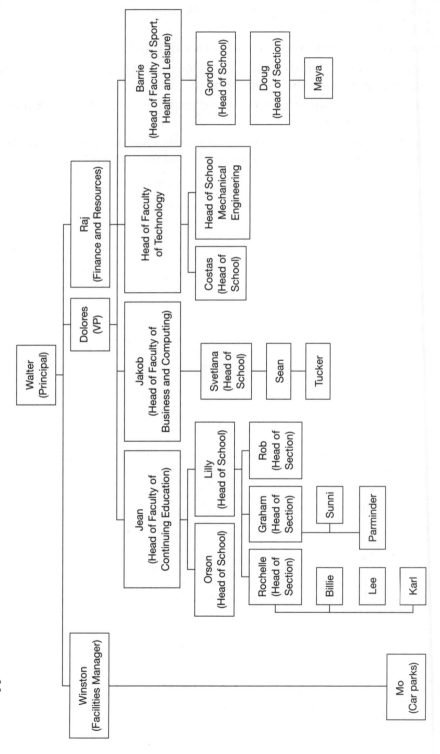

References and further reading

ACM (2004) *The reflective college manager*, Leicester: ACM.

Adair, J (1983) *Effective leadership*, London: Gower.

Alderfer, C P (1972) *Existence, relatedness and growth: human needs in organizational settings*, New York: Free Press.

Anderson, R (Undated) *Mastering Leadership*, website article **www.theleadershipcircle.com** (last accessed 14/9/2006).

Barrett, R (1998) *Liberating the corporate soul*, Boston, MA: Butterworth Heinemann.

Bass, B M and Avolio, B J (1994) *Improving organisational effectiveness through transformational leadership*, Thousand Oaks, CA: Sage Publications.

Bennett, N, Crawford, M and Cartwright, M (eds) (2003) *Effective education leadership*, Oxford: Oxford University Press.

Bennis, W G (1989) *On becoming a leader*, London, Random House.

Bennis, W G (2004) *Competencies of exemplary leadership*, Keynote speech at CIPD Conference.

Bennis, W G and Nanus, B (1985) *Leaders: strategies for taking charge*, New York: Harper & Row.

Bennis, W G and Powell, S (2000) Great groups and leaders, *Career Development International*, 5 (2), 112–15.

Bennis, W G and Thomas, R J (2002) *Geeks and geezers*, Boston, MA: Harvard Business School Press.

Blanchard, K, Zigarmi, P and Zigarmi, D (1986) *Leadership and the one-minute manager*, London: HarperCollins.

Bolman, L and Deal, T (1993) *Reframing organisations: artistry, choice and leadership*, San Francisco, CA: Jossey-Bass.

Bridges, W (1991) *Managing transitions*. Reading, Mass: Perseus.

Briggs, A (2001) Academic middle managers in further education: reflections on leadership, *Research in Post-Compulsory Education*, 6 (2), 223–36.

Briggs, A R J and Middlewood, D (2005), *Leadership, development and diversity in the learning and skills sector*, London: Learning and Skills Research Centre.

Chandler, D G (1973) *Campaigns of Napoleon: the mind and method of history's greatest soldier*, New York: Scribner.

Collins, J (2001) *Good to great*, London: Random House.

Collins, J C and Porras, J I (1994) *Built to last*, London: Random House.

Conger, J (2004), Developing leadership capability: what's inside the black box?, *Academy of Management Executive*, 18 (3), 136–9.

Covey, S (1989) *The seven habits of highly effective people*, London: Simon & Schuster.

Craner, T (2004) *Leadership in SMEs: organisational vision for innovation,* Warwick University, International Automotive Research Centre.

Cronin, V (1990) *Napoleon*, New York: HarperCollins.

De Bono, E (1985) *Six thinking hats*, London: Penguin.

DfES (2006) *Further education: raising skills, improving life chances*, London: The Stationery Office.

Drucker, P F (2001) *The essential Drucker*, Woburn, MA: Butterworth-Heinemann.

Eales-White, R (1992) Leading into a Successful Future, *Industrial and Commercial Training*, 24 (7), 19–25.

Firth, D (1999) *Smart things to know about change*, Oxford: Capstone.

Foster, A (2005) *Realising the potential: a review of the future role of further education colleges*, London: The Stationery Office.

Frost, P J (2003) *Toxic emotions at work*, Boston, Mass: Harvard Business School Press.

Gladwell, M (2000) *The tipping point*, London: Little, Brown.

Goffee, R and Jones, G (2000) Why should anyone be led by you?, *Harvard Business Review*, 78 (5), 62–70.

Goleman, D, Boyatzis, R and McKee, A (2002) *The new leaders*, London: Little, Brown.

Gravells, J M (2006) The myth of change management: a reflection on personal change and its lessons for leadership development, *Human Resources Development International*, 9, (2) 283–9.

Grint, K (1999) The arts of leadership, in Bennett, N, Crawford, M, and Cartwright, M, (ed) *Effective educational leadership*, Oxford: Oxford University Press.

Heifetz, R A and Laurie, D L (2001) The work of leadership, *Harvard Business Review*, 75, January–February, 124–34.

Herrmann, N (1996) *The whole brain business book*, New York: McGraw-Hill.

Herzberg, F (1966) *Work and the nature of man*, Cleveland, OH: World Publishing.

Higgs, M and Rowland, D (2005) All changes great and small: exploring approaches to change and its leadership. *Journal of Change Management*, 5 (2), 121–51.

Hooper, A and Potter, J (2000) *Intelligent leadership*, London: Random House Business Books.

Hutchinson, S, Kinnie, N and Purcell, J (2003) *HR practices and business performance: what makes a difference?* University of Bath School of Management Work and Employment Research Centre Working Paper Series 2003.10.

Immerwahr J (1983) *Putting the work ethic to work*, New York: Public Agenda Foundation.

Jameson, J (2006) *Leadership in post-compulsory education*, London: David Fulton.

Judge, T A and Bono, J E (2000) Five-factor model of personality and transformational leadership, *Journal of Applied Psychology*, 85, 751–65.

Kanter, R (1984) *The change masters*, New York: Touchstone Books.

Kaplan, R S and Norton, D P (1993) Putting the balanced scorecard to work, *Harvard Business Review*, 71 (5), 134–7.

Kelman, S (2000) Making change, *Government Executive*, 32 (1), 28.

Kets de Vries, M (2001) Leadership group coaching in action – the Zen of creating high performance teams. *Academy of Management Executive*, 19 (1), 61–76.

Kets de Vries, M (2001) *The leadership mystique*, Harlow: Pearson Education.

Kim, W C and Mauborgne, R and van der Heyden, L (2002) General failings, *Financial Times*, 6 December.

Kim, W C and Mauborgne, R (2003) Tipping point leadership. *Harvard Business Review*, 81 (4), 60–9.

Kotter, J P (1996) *Leading change*, Boston, Mass: Harvard Business School Press.

Kouzes, J W and Posner, B Z (1995) *The leadership challenge*, San Francisco, CA: Jossey-Bass.

LLUK (2005) *National Occupational Standards for Leadership and Management in the Post-Compulsory Learning and Skills Sector*, London: LLUK.

LSDA (2003) *Leadership and management survey*, London: LSDA.

Luhmann, N (1979) *Trust and power*, Chichester: John Wiley & Sons.

Lumby, J and Tomlinson, H (2000) Principals speaking: managerialism and leadership in further education, *Research in Post-Compulsory Education*, 5 (2), 139–51.

Lumby, J, Harris, A, Morrison, M, Muijs, D, Sood, K, Glover, D, Wilson, M, Briggs, ARJ, and Middlewood, D (2005) *Leadership, development and diversity in the learning and skills sector*, London: Learning and Skills Research Centre.

Lygo, R (1996) Sir Raymond Lygo on Leadership, in Crainer, S (ed) *Leaders on leadership – twelve personal reflections on the theme of leadership*, Corby: Institute of Management, p78.

Manzoni, J-F and Barsoux, J-L (2002) *The set-up to fail syndrome: how good managers cause great people to fail*, Boston MA: Harvard Business School Press.

Maslow, A H (1962) *Toward a psychology of being*, New York: Van Nostrand.

Morrell, M and Capparell, S (2001) *Shackleton's way*, London: Nicholas Brealey Publishing.

Morris, L (1996) Employees not encouraged to go extra mile, *Training and Development*, 50 (4), p59.

Nash, I (2006) 'Caught in the middle of a mess', *Times Educational Supplement FE Focus*, 7 July 2006, p5.

Nohria, N, Joyce, W and Robertson, B (2003) What really works, *Harvard Business Review*, 81 (7) pp43–52.

Parker, P (1996) Sir Peter Parker on Leadership, in Crainer, S (ed) *Leaders on leadership – twelve personal reflections on the theme of leadership*, Corby: Institute of Management, p33.

Pass, S (2004) *Looking inside the 'Black Box': employee opinions of HRM/HPWS and organisational performance*, British Universities Industrial Relations Association Annual Conference, Nottingham University, UK.

Pounder, L (2005) Letter, in *People Management*, March, p22.

Ready, D A (1993) *Champions of change*, Lexington, MA: International Consortium for Executive Development Research.

Rubin, R S, Munz, D C and Bommer, W H (2005) Leading from within: the effects of emotion recognition and personality on transformational leadership behaviour, *Academy of Management Journal*, 43 (5), 845–53.

Schein, E (1969) *Process consultation: its role in organisation development*, Reading, MA: Addison Wesley Publishing.

Schein, E (1992) *Organisational culture and leadership*, San Francisco, CA: Jossey-Bass.

Senge, P (1990) *The fifth discipline*, London: Random House.

SVUK (2006) 'New professional standards: teacher/tutor/trainer education for the learning and skills sector' (draft).

Usher, R and Edwards, R (1994) *Postmodernism and education*, London: Routledge.

Van Maurik, J (2001) *Writers on leadership*, London: Penguin.

Wallace, S and Gravells, J (2007) Professional Development in the Lifelong Learning Sector: *Mentoring in Further Education* (2nd edition), Exeter: Learning Matters.

Wallace, S and Gravells, J (2006) *A–Z for Every Manager in FE*, London: Continuum.

Wells, R (1996) Richard Wells on Leadership, in Crainer, S (ed) *Leaders on leadership – twelve personal reflections on the theme of leadership*, Corby: Institute of Management, p99.

West, M A (1994) *Effective teamwork*, Oxford: BPS Blackwell.

Wiseman, R (2003) *The luck factor*, London: Arrow Books.

Withers, B (2000) The Evolution of the Role of Principal in Further Education: a follow-up study, in *Research in Post-Compulsory Education*, 5 (3), 371–89.

Yankelovich, Daniel and Associates (1983) *Work and human values*, New York: Public Agenda Foundation.

Young, T L (1998) *The handbook of project management*, London: Kogan Page.

Index

Added to the page number 'f' denotes a figure and 't' denotes a table.

accessibility 9
accountability 82
action
   learning from 90
   see also corrective action
Action Centred Leadership 84
action planning
   agreeing objectives for 76
   prioritising and 63–4
adaptive capacity, building 97, 102
'adaptive leadership' 13, 110
ambiguity, handling 100, 102
approachability 26–7
attitude 30
authenticity 26, 110

'balanced scorecards' 86
big, hairy, audacious goals 48
Blanchard's Situational Leadership Model 92
'born or made' argument 7–8, 10, 68
brutal facts, confronting 22, 97
building tasks 85
Built to last 48
'butterfly syndrome' 109t

capabilities
   leadership 85
   see also creating capability
caring 28
change
   external agents 105, 106
   framework 115f
   instinct for 13
   leadership responsibilities 110
   leading 105–18
      'now' 116
      teams 110–18
      'the future' 117–18
      'the new normal' 117
      'the past' 116
      'the unknown' 116–17
   linear approaches 107–8
change fatigue 105–10
   consequences 107–8
      responses to 108–10
circle of influence 96
clarity 9
classical perfection and the competence model of
      leadership 11–12, 16
cloning and the competence model of leadership
      11, 14
coaching 12, 71
coaching leadership style 92
cognitive hurdle 87

collaboration 84
'collaborative' leadership 17
common sense approach to leadership 11, 15–16
communication 21–2
   setting up 86
   and supporting professional development 76
compelling stories, telling see telling compelling
      stories
competence 29
competence model of leadership 18
   and the 'born or made' argument 10
   criteria 9–10
   drawbacks 10–16
      classical perfection 12, 16
      cloning 11, 14
      common sense 11, 15–16
      comprehensiveness 12–13
conflict, handling 88–90
congruence 26
connecting with people 13, 20–34, 41, 53, 116, 117
   and competence and expertise 29
   the 'dark side' 32
   demonstrating trust and respect 27–8
   and enthusiasm, conviction and passion 30–1
   and fairness and decency 27
   and honesty, authenticity and integrity 26
   importance of 21–4
   issues for the Lifelong Learning sector 32
   self-evaluation and development 33–4
   and visibility and approachability 27
consistency 9, 26
'constructive conflict', encouraging 90
continual intervention 105
control
   balancing freedom and 82–3
   over change 105–6, 107
conviction 30
corrective action, taking 87
CPD (continuing professional development) 3, 36
   see also professional development
creating capability 67–80
   the 'dark side' 78
   issues for Lifelong Learning 79
   and modelling good practice 68–70
   self-evaluation and development 79
   and steps to support professional development
      see professional development, steps to
      support
   and supporting professional development of
      teams 78
credibility, achieving 21–4
'critical success factors', identification 86
culture of discipline 85

data
    importance of 82
    looking at 86
    reporting 86
decency 27
decision-making, distributed 84
delegating leadership style 92
Department for Education and Skills (DfES) 106
development
    of others 116, 117
    see also CPD (continuing professional
        development); professional development;
        self-development; team development
directive leadership style 92
discretionary effort 21
distance, balance between approachability and 27
distributed decision-making 84
distributed leadership 79
    moving from transactional to 81

emotional intelligence 13, 25, 40
empowerment 28
enthusiasm 30
environment, interpreting 36–41
ethical dimension see 'moral compass'
expertise 29, 30

fairness 27
feedback
    360 degree 33
    giving 12
        constructive 77
    seeking and responding to 62–3
    and self-evaluation 33
'first-class noticers' 39, 41
Foster Report (2005) 2, 42, 54
'four whys' technique 55
Framework for Excellence, Learning and Skills
        Council (LSC) 3
freedom, balancing control and 82–3
Further education: raising skills, improving life
        chances 2–3, 9, 42, 71

getting on the balcony 39
goals
    reviewing outcomes against 77
    see also big, hairy, audacious goals
good practice, modelling 68–70
'guardian' role 97–8

honesty 26
hunches, following 95, 96
hurdles, identifying and addressing 87–8

idealised influence 25
incorporation in further education (FE) 8
induction 74, 75f
influence
    achieving 21–5
    circle of 96
informal, social contact, space for 28

information sharing 21–2, 28
inspirational motivation 46
instinct for opportunity 13, 35–44, 116, 117
    the 'dark side' 42
    and interpreting the environment 36–41
    issues for the Lifelong Learning sector 42
    self-evaluation and development 42–3
integrity 26
interpersonal skills 21, 22
    training programmes 34

joined-up leadership 119–31
    whole-college issues 124–31

leaders
    'born or made' argument 7–8, 10, 68
    what is 'core' about 52–3
    see also perfect leaders
leadership
    Action Centred Leadership 84
    adaptive leadership 13, 110
    Blanchard's situation leadership model 92
    coaching leadership style 92
    collaborative leadership 17
    common sense approach to leadership 11, 15–16
    competence model see competence model of
        leadership
    delegating leadership style 92
    directive leadership style 92
    distinction between management and 83
    distributed leadership 79
    level five leadership 97
    styles of 17
        'correct' 4
    supporting leadership style 92
    transactional leadership 25, 81
    transformational leadership 13, 46, 81
leadership capabilities 85
leadership framework 104f
leadership issues 3–4
Leadership and Management Standards see
        Occupational Standards for Leadership and
        Management
leading by example 68–70
learning from taking action 90
'learning on the job' 8
Learning and Skills Council (LSC) 106
    Framework for Excellence 3
'let go', knowing when to 100
Level Five leadership 97
Lifelong Learning UK (LLUK) 106
    Standards for Leadership and Management see
        Occupational Standards for Leadership and
        Management
linear approaches to change 108
listening 22, 26
loyalty, inspiring 12
luck, making your own 95–6
The luck factor 95

maintenance tasks 85
making things happen 81–93, 116, 117
    the 'dark side' 91
    and freedom or control 82–3
    and handling conflict 88–90
    and helping others to be more effective 85–7
    issues for the Lifelong Learning sector 91
    learning from taking action 90–1
    self-evaluation and development 92
    squaring the circle 84–5
    and techniques of leadership 87–8
management, distinction between leadership and
        83
managerialism 32
'mavens' 39
meaning in leadership 46–7
mentoring 62, 70–5
    model 74f
micro-management by politicians 105
milestones, setting 86
misfortune, conversion into success 96
mission 45
    creating a sense of 46
    meaning 47
    and moral and ethical direction 54
modelling good practice 68–70
monitoring performance 75–6
'moral compass' 2, 19
    and connecting with people 32
    and creating capability 79
    and instinct for opportunity 41–2
    and making things happen 90–1
    and reflective leadership 64
    and staying positive 100–1
    and telling compelling stories 54
    values as an element 47
motivational hurdle 88
motivational theory 46

objectives
    agreeing 76, 85
    SMART 86
Occupational Standards for Leadership and
        Management 2, 8
    and competent leadership see competence model
        of leadership
    and instinct for opportunity 35
    and making things happen 82
    and seeking and responding to feedback 63
    and staying positive 95
    and team development 78
    and vision 52
openness 21–2
    and honesty, authenticity and integrity 26
    and visibility and approachability 26–7
opportunities
    instinct for see instinct for opportunity
    maximising 95, 96
optimism 95, 96
organisational values, fit between personal and 52
outcomes 127
    reviewing 77

passion 30
passivity, avoiding 100
PAT 70
people skills see connecting with people
perfect leaders 12, 16
performance
    leadership 2
    monitoring 75–6
performance 'dashboards' 86
personal values, fit between organisational and 52
personal values inventories 55
personality questionnaires 33
pinch of reality 98
'plugging the gaps' approach 15
polarisation 112–13
policy, current context 3
political hurdle 88
politicians, micro-management by 105
positive, staying see staying positive
practice
    current context 3
    see also good practice
prioritising and action planning 63–4
professional development 8–9
    and prioritising and action planning 63–4
    steps to support 70, 74–7
        agreeing objectives 76
        communication 76
        monitoring performance 75–6
        negotiating support 77
        provision of induction 75, 75f
        reviewing outcomes against goals and giving
            constructive feedback 77
    see also CPD (continuing professional
        development); self-development; team
        development
professional ethics see 'moral compass'
professionalisation 10
progress, tracking 87
psychometric tests 33
purpose 47, 85
    common 47
    creating 48–51
'Pygmalion Effect' 78

Quality Improvement Agency (QIA) initiatives 3

Raising skills, improving life chances 2–3, 9, 42, 71
reading situations 37
reality, exposure to 97
recognition 15
reflective development through action 67f
reflective journals 58
    examples of entries 59–61
reflective leadership 57–66
    the 'dark side' 64
    issues for Lifelong Learning 64–5
    and managing your time effectively 64
    and prioritising and action planning 63–4
    and seeking and responding to feedback 62–3
    self-evaluation and development 65
reflective practice 58–61
    model 59f